BLACK&DECKER®

HERE'S HOW...
DECKS

Build Your Very Own Deck
in 12 Easy Steps

Creative Publishing
international

MINNEAPOLIS, MINNESOTA

www.creativepub.com

Contents

Building Decks
A Step-by-Step Overview

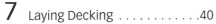

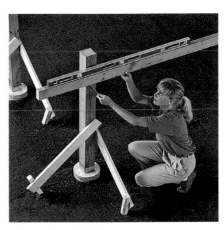

Building Decks: A Step-by-step Overview

Deck-building is a project you'll tackle in stages, no matter what design you choose. Before you begin construction, review the photos on these two pages. They outline the basic procedure you'll want to follow when building your deck. The chapters to follow will explore each of these stages extensively.

Be sure to gather your tools and materials before you begin the project, and arrange to have a helper available for the more difficult stages. Check with local utilities for the location of underground electrical, telephone, or water lines before digging the footings. Apply for a building permit, where required, and make sure a building inspector has approved the deck design before beginning work.

The time it takes to build a deck depends on the size and complexity of the design as well as your building skills. If you're comfortable using tools and start with thorough, accurate plans, you should be able to complete a single-level deck in a few weekends.

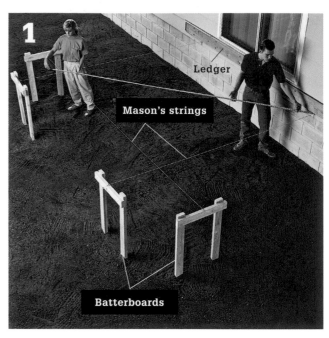

Install a ledger to anchor the deck to the house and to serve as reference for laying out footings (pages 6 to 13). Use batterboards and mason's strings to locate footings, and check for square by measuring diagonals (page 17).

Pour concrete post footings (pages 20 to 23), and install metal post anchors (pages 25 to 26). Set and brace the posts, attach them to the post anchors, and mark posts to show where beam will be attached (pages 26 to 29).

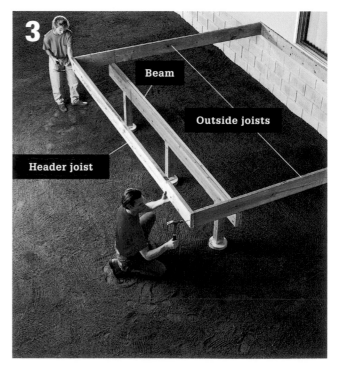

Fasten the beam to the posts (pages 30 to 33). Install the outside joists and header joist, using galvanized nails (pages 35 to 36).

Install metal joist hangers on the ledger and header joist, then hang the remaining joists (pages 36 to 39). Most decking patterns require joists that are spaced 16" on center.

Lay decking boards, and trim them with a circular saw (pages 40 to 49). If desired for appearance, cover pressure-treated header and outside joists with redwood or cedar facing boards (page 42).

Build deck stairs. Stairs provide access to the deck and establish traffic patterns.

Install a railing around the deck and stairway (page 68). A railing adds a decorative touch and may be required on any deck that is more than 30" above the ground. If desired, finish the underside of the deck.

1. Installing a Ledger

The first step in building an attached deck is to fasten the ledger to the house. The ledger anchors the deck and establishes a reference point for building the deck square and level. The ledger also supports one end of all the deck joists, so it must be attached securely to the framing members of the house.

If your deck's ledger is made from pressure-treated lumber, make sure to use hot-dipped, galvanized lag screws and washers to attach it to the house. Ordinary zinc-coated hardware will corrode and eventually fail if placed in contact with ACQ pressure-treating chemicals.

Install the ledger so that the surface of the decking boards will be 1" below the indoor floor level. This height difference prevents rainwater or melted snow from seeping into the house.

Tools & Materials

Pencil
Level
Circular saw with carbide blade
Chisel
Hammer
Metal snips
Caulk gun
Drill and bits
   (¼" twist, 1" spade, ⅜" and ⅝" masonry)
Ratchet wrench
Awl
Rubber mallet
Pressure-treated lumber
Galvanized flashing
8d galvanized common nails
Silicone caulk
⅜ × 4" lag screws and 1" washers
Lead masonry anchors for ⅜" lag screws
   (for brick walls)
2 × 4s for braces

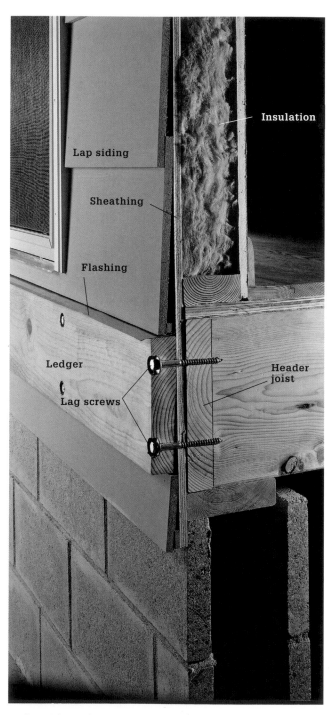

Ledger (shown in cross section) is made from pressure-treated lumber. Lap siding is cut away to expose sheathing and to provide a flat surface for attaching the ledger. Galvanized flashing tucked under siding prevents moisture damage to wood. Countersunk ⅜ × 4" lag screws hold ledger to header joist inside house. If there is access to the space behind the header joist, such as in an unfinished basement, attach the ledger with carriage bolts, washers, and nuts.

How to Attach a Ledger to Lap Siding

Draw an outline showing where the deck will fit against the house, using a level as a guide. Include the thickness of the outside joists and any decorative facing boards that will be installed.

Cut out siding along outline, using a circular saw. Set blade depth to same thickness as siding, so that blade does not cut into sheathing.

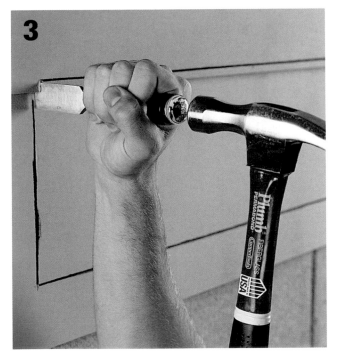

Use a chisel to finish the cutout where circular saw blade does not reach. Hold the chisel with the bevel-side in.

Measure and cut ledger from pressure-treated lumber. Remember that ledger will be shorter than overall length of cutout.

(continued)

5

Cut galvanized flashing to length of cutout, using metal snips. Slide flashing up under siding. Do not nail the metal flashing in place.

6

Center the ledger in the cutout, underneath the flashing. Brace in position, and tack ledger into place with 8d galvanized nails. Apply a thick bead of silicone caulk to crack between siding and flashing.

7

Drill pairs of ¼" pilot holes spaced every 2 feet, through the ledger and sheathing and into the header joist.

8

Counterbore each pilot hole to ½" depth, using a 1" spade bit.

9

Attach ledger to wall with ⅜ × 4" lag screws and washers, using a ratchet wrench or impact driver.

10

Seal lag screw heads with silicone caulk. Seal the crack between the wall and the sides and bottom of the ledger.

How to Attach a Ledger to Masonry

1

Measure and cut ledger. Ledger will be shorter than overall length of outline. Drill pairs of ¼" pilot holes every 2 feet in ledger. Counterbore each pilot hole to ½" depth, using a 1" spade bit.

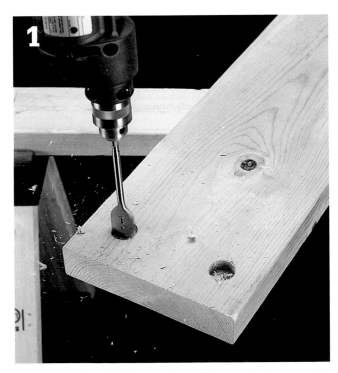

2

Draw an outline of the deck on the wall, using a level as a guide. Center ledger in outline on wall, and brace in position. Mark the pilot hole locations on wall, using an awl or nail. Remove ledger.

(continued)

Drill anchor holes 3" deep into masonry, using a ⅝" masonry bit.

Drive lead masonry anchors for ⅜" lag screws into drilled holes, using a rubber mallet.

Attach ledger to wall with ⅜ × 4" lag screws and washers, using a ratchet wrench or impact driver. Tighten screws firmly, but do not overtighten.

Seal the cracks between the wall and ledger with silicone caulk. Also seal the lag screw heads.

How to Attach a Ledger to Stucco

Draw outline of deck on wall, using a level as a guide. Measure and cut ledger, and drill pilot holes (page 9, step 1). Brace ledger against wall, and mark hole locations, using a nail or awl.

Remove ledger. Drill pilot holes through stucco layer of wall, using a ⅜" masonry bit.

Extend each pilot hole through the sheathing and into the header joist, using a ¼" bit. Reposition ledger and brace in place.

Attach ledger to wall with ⅜ × 4" lag screws and washers, using a ratchet wrench. Seal the lag screw heads and the cracks between the wall and ledger with silicone caulk.

How to Attach a Ledger to Metal or Vinyl Siding

Deck height, finished

Outside of deck

Lower cutout mark

Mark the length of the ledger location, adding 1½" at each end to allow for the rim joists that will be installed later. Also allow for fascia board thickness if it will be added and create space for metal rim-joist hangers. Then mark the top and bottom edges of the ledger at both ends of its location. Snap lines for the ledger position between the marks. Check the lines for level and adjust as necessary. You may be able to use the siding edges to help determine the ledger location, but only after checking to see if the edges are level. Don't assume siding is installed level.

Set the circular saw blade depth to cut through the siding. Use a metal cutting blade for metal siding; a 40-tooth carbide blade works well on vinyl siding. Cut on the outside of the lines along the top and sides of the ledger location, stopping the blade when it reaches a corner.

Snap a new level line ½" above the bottom line and make your final cut along this line. This leaves a small lip of siding that will fit under the ledger.

4

Complete the cuts in the corners, using tin snips on metal siding or a utility knife on vinyl siding. A hammer and sharp chisel also may be used.

5

Insert building felt underneath the siding and over the existing felt that has been damaged by the cuts. It is easiest to cut and install two long strips. Cut and insert the first strip so it is underneath the siding at the ends and bottom edge of the cutout and attach it with staples. Cut and insert the second strip so it is underneath the siding at the ends and top edge of the cutout, so that it overlaps the first strip by at least 3".

6

Cut and insert galvanized flashing (also called Z-flashing) underneath the full length of the top edge of the cutout. Do not use fasteners; pressure will hold the flashing in place until the ledger is installed.

7

Cut and install the ledger board (see pages 7 to 9).

2. Locating Post Footings

Establish the exact locations of all concrete footings by stretching mason's strings across the site. Use the ledger board as a starting point. These perpendicular layout strings will be used to locate holes for concrete footings and to position metal post anchors on the finished footings. Anchor the layout strings with temporary 2 × 4 supports, often called batterboards. You may want to leave the batterboards in place until after the footings are dug. That way, you can use the strings to accurately locate the J-bolts in the concrete.

Tools & Materials

Tape measure	Line level
Felt-tipped pen	Plumb bob
Circular saw	2 × 4s
Screwgun	10d nails
Framing square	2½" wallboard screws
Masonry hammer	Mason's strings
Claw hammer	Masking tape

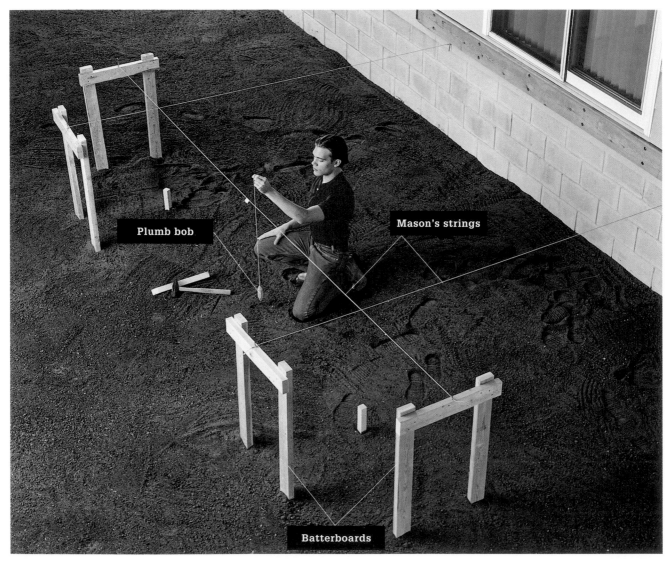

Plumb bob

Mason's strings

Batterboards

Mason's strings stretched between ledger and batterboards are used to position footings for deck posts. Use a plumb bob and stakes to mark the ground at the exact centerpoints of footings.

How to Locate Post Footings

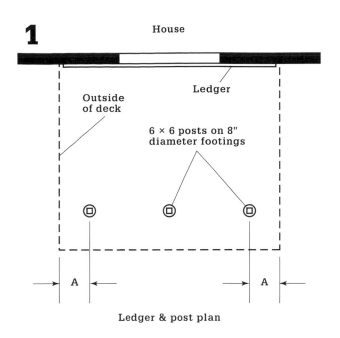

Use your design plan to find distance (A). Measure from the side of the deck to the center of each outside post. Use your elevation drawings to find the height of each deck post.

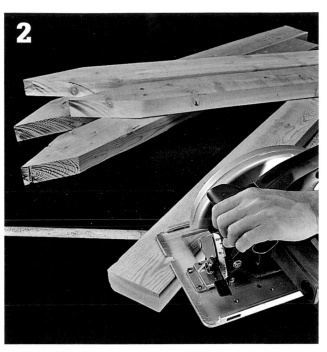

Cut 2 × 4 stakes for batterboards, each about 8" longer than post height. Trim one end of each stake to a point, using a circular saw. Cut 2 × 4 crosspieces, each about 2 feet long.

Assemble batterboards by attaching crosspieces to stakes with 2½" wallboard screws. Crosspieces should be about 2" below tops of stakes.

Transfer measurement A (step 1) to ledger, and mark reference points at each end of ledger. String lines will be stretched from these points on ledger. When measuring, remember to allow for outside joists and facing that will be butted to the ends of the ledger.

(continued)

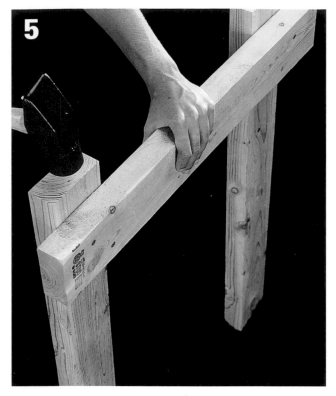

Drive a batterboard 6" into the ground, about 2 feet past the post location. Crosspiece of batterboard should be parallel to the ledger.

Drive a 10d nail into bottom of ledger at reference point (step 4). Attach a mason's string to nail.

Extend the mason's string so that it is taut and perpendicular to the ledger. Use a framing square as a guide. Secure the string temporarily by wrapping it several times around the batterboard.

Check the mason's string for square using "3-4-5 carpenter's triangle." First, measure along the ledger 3 feet from the mason's string and mark a point, using a felt-tipped pen.

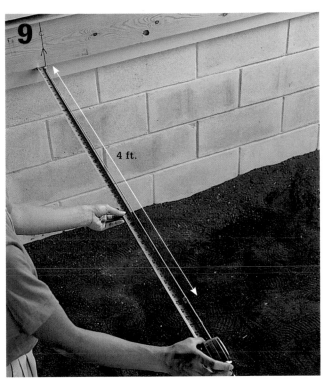

Measure mason's string 4 feet from edge of ledger, and mark with masking tape.

Measure distance between marks. If string is perpendicular to ledger, the distance will be exactly 5 feet. If necessary, move string left or right on batterboard until distance between marks is 5 feet.

Drive a 10d nail into top of batterboard at string location. Leave about 2" of nail exposed. Tie string to nail.

(continued)

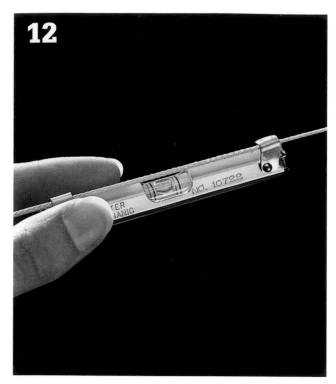

Hang a line level on the mason's string. Raise or lower string until it is level. Locate other outside post footing, repeating steps 5 to 12.

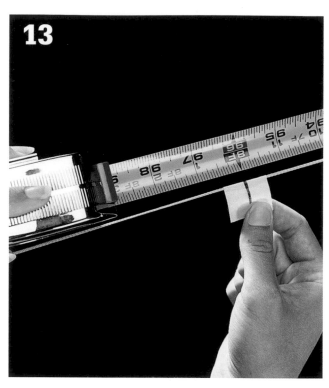

Measure along mason's strings from ledger to find centerpoint of posts. Mark centerpoints on strings, using masking tape.

Drive additional batterboards into ground, about 2 feet outside mason's strings and lined up with post centerpoint marks (step 13).

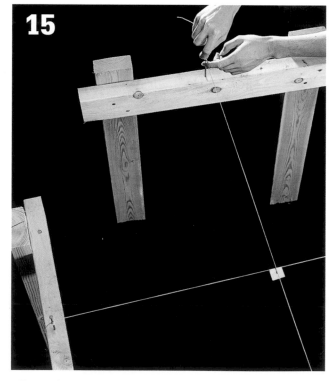

Align a third cross string with the centerpoint marks on the first strings. Drive 10d nails in new batterboards, and tie off cross string on nails. Cross string should be close to, but not touching, the first strings.

16

Check strings for square by measuring distances A-B and C-D. Measure diagonals A-D and B-C from edge of ledger to opposite corners. If strings are square, measurement A-B will be same as C-D, and diagonal A-D will be same as B-C. If necessary, adjust strings on batterboards until square.

17

Measure along the cross string and mark centerpoints of any posts that will be installed between the outside posts.

18

Use a plumb bob to mark post centerpoints on the ground, directly under the marks on the mason's strings. Drive a stake into ground at each point. Remove mason's strings before digging footings.

3. Digging & Pouring Footings

Concrete footings hold deck posts in place and support the weight of the deck. Check local codes to determine the size and depth of footings required for your area. In cold climates, footings must be deeper than the soil frost line.

To help protect posts from water damage, each footing should be poured so that it is 2" above ground level. Tube-shaped forms let you extend the footings above ground level.

It is easy and inexpensive to mix your own concrete by combining portland cement, sand, gravel, and water.

As an alternative to inserting J-bolts into wet concrete, you can use masonry anchors, or install anchor bolts with an epoxy designed for deck footings and other masonry installations. The epoxy method provides you with more time to reset layout strings for locating bolt locations, and it eliminates the problem of J-bolts tilting or sinking into concrete that is too loose. Most building centers sell threaded rod, washers, nuts, and epoxy syringes, but you also can buy these items separately at most hardware centers.

Before digging, consult local utilities for location of any underground electrical, telephone, or water lines that might interfere with footings.

Tools & Materials

Power auger
  or clamshell
  posthole digger
Tape measure
Pruning saw
Shovel
Reciprocating saw
  or handsaw
Torpedo level
Hoe
Trowel
Shovel
Old toothbrush
Plumb bob
Utility knife

Concrete tube forms
Portland cement
Sand
Gravel
J-bolts
Wheelbarrow
Scrap 2 × 4

Power augers quickly dig holes for post footings. They are available at rental centers. Some models can be operated by one person, while others require two people.

How to Dig & Pour Post Footings

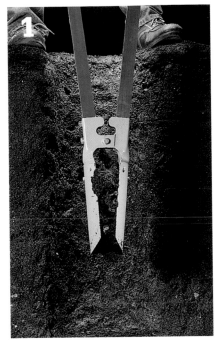

Dig holes for post footings with a clamshell digger or power auger, centering the holes on the layout stakes. For holes deeper than 35", use a power auger.

Measure hole depth. Local building codes specify depth of footings. Cut away tree roots, if necessary, using a pruning saw.

Pour 2" to 3" of loose gravel in the bottom of each footing hole. Gravel will provide drainage under concrete footings.

Add 2" to hole depth so that footings will be above ground level. Cut concrete tube forms to length, using a reciprocating saw or handsaw. Make sure cuts are straight.

Insert tubes into footing holes, leaving about 2" of tube above ground level. Use a level to make sure tops of tubes are level. Pack soil around tubes to hold them in place.

(continued)

Mix dry ingredients for concrete in a wheelbarrow, using a hoe.

Form a hollow in center of dry concrete mixture. Slowly pour a small amount of water into hollow, and blend in dry mixture with a hoe.

Add more water gradually, mixing thoroughly until concrete is firm enough to hold its shape when sliced with a trowel.

Pour concrete slowly into the tube form, guiding concrete from the wheelbarrow with a shovel. Fill about half of the form, using a long stick to tamp the concrete, filling any air gaps in the footing. Then finish pouring and tamping concrete into the form.

Level the concrete by pulling a 2 × 4 across the top of the tube form, using a sawing motion. Add concrete to any low spots. Retie the mason's strings on the batterboards, and recheck measurements.

Insert a J-bolt at an angle into the wet concrete at center of the footing.

Lower the J-bolt slowly into the concrete, wiggling it slightly to eliminate any air gaps.

Set the J-bolt so ¾" to 1" is exposed above concrete. Brush away any wet concrete on bolt threads with an old toothbrush.

Use a plumb bob to make sure the J-bolt is positioned exactly at center of post location.

Use a torpedo level to make sure the J-bolt is plumb. If necessary, adjust the bolt and repack concrete. Let concrete cure, then cut away exposed portion of tube with a utility knife.

4. Installing Posts

Posts support the deck beams and transfer the weight of the deck, as well as everything on it, to the concrete footings. They create the above-ground foundation of your deck. Your building inspector will verify that the posts you plan to use are sized correctly to suit your deck design.

Choose post lumber carefully so the posts will be able to carry these substantial loads for the life of your deck. Pressure-treated lumber is your best defense against rot or insect damage. Select posts that are straight and free of deep cracks, large knots, or other natural defects that could compromise their strength. Try not to cut off the factory-treated ends when trimming the posts to length; they contain more of the treatment chemicals and generally last longer than cut ends. Face the factory ends down against the post hardware where water is more likely to accumulate.

Use galvanized metal post anchors to attach the posts to concrete footings. If posts are set directly on concrete, the ends won't dry properly. You'll also have a harder time making the necessary mechanical connection to the footings. Post anchors have drainage holes and pedestals that raise the ends of the wood above the footings and improve drainage. Make sure the posts are installed plumb for maximum strength.

Tools & Materials

Pencil
Framing square
Ratchet wrench
Tape measure
Power miter saw or circular saw
Hammer
Screwgun
Level
Combination square
Metal post anchors
Nuts for J-bolts
Lumber for posts
6d galvanized common nails
2" wallboard screws
Long, straight 2 × 4
1 × 4s
Pointed 2 × 2 stakes

How to Attach Post Anchors

Mark the top of each footing as a reference line for installing post anchors. Lay a long, straight 2 × 4 flat across two or three concrete footings, parallel to the ledger, with one edge tight against the J-bolts.

Draw a reference line across each concrete footing, using an edge of the 2 × 4 as a guide. Remove the 2 × 4.

Place a metal post anchor on each concrete footing, and center it over the J-bolt.

(continued)

Use a framing square to make sure the post anchor is positioned square to the reference line drawn on the footing.

Thread a nut over each J-bolt, and tighten it securely with a ratchet wrench or impact driver.

How to Set Posts

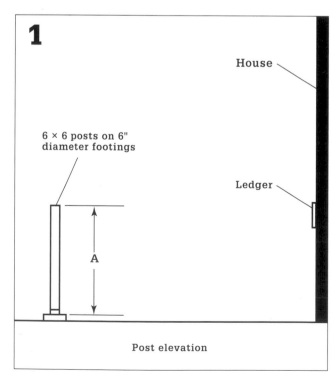

1

6 × 6 posts on 6" diameter footings

House

Ledger

A

Post elevation

Use the elevation drawing from your design plan to find the length of each post (A). Add 6" for a cutting margin.

Cut posts with power miter saw or circular saw. Make sure factory-treated ends of posts are square. If necessary, square them by trimming with a power miter saw or circular saw.

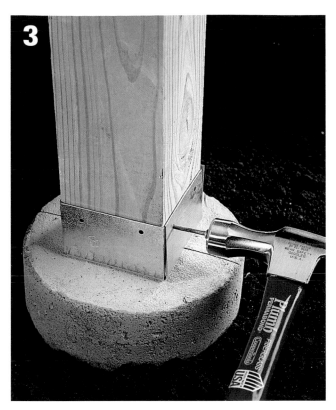

Place post in anchor, and tack into place with a single 6d galvanized common nail.

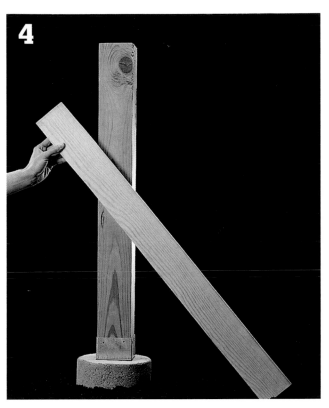

Brace post with a 1 × 4. Place the 1 × 4 flat across post so that it crosses the post at a 45° angle about halfway up.

Attach the brace to the post temporarily with a single 2" wallboard screw.

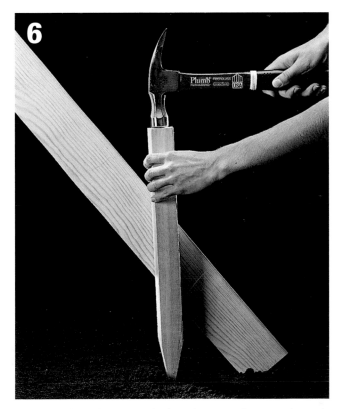

Drive a pointed 2 × 2 stake into the ground next to the end of the brace.

(continued)

Use a level to make sure the post is plumb. Adjust the post, if necessary.

Attach the brace to the stake with two 2" wallboard screws.

Plumb and brace the post on the side perpendicular to the first brace.

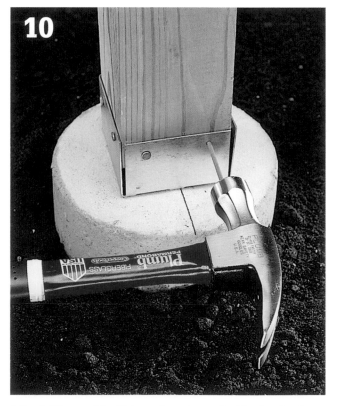

Attach the post to the post anchor with 6d galvanized common nails.

11

Position a straight 2 × 4 with one end on the ledger and the other end across the face of the post. Level the 2 × 4, then lower its post end ¼" for every 3 ft. between the ledger and the post (for water runoff). Draw a line on the post along the bottom of the 2 × 4. This line indicates the top of the joists.

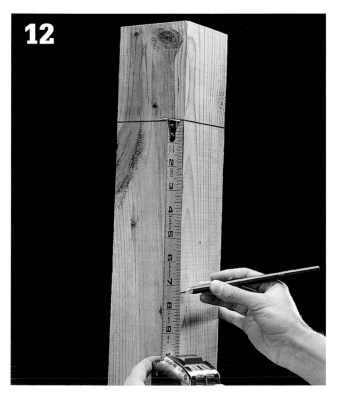

12

From the line shown in step 11, measure down and mark the posts a distance equal to the width of the joists.

13

Use a square to draw a line completely around the post. This line indicates the top of the beam. From this line, repeat steps 12 and 13 to determine the bottom of the beam.

5. Installing Beams

Deck beams attach to the posts to help support the weight of the joists and decking. Installation methods depend on the deck design and local codes, so check with a building inspector to determine what is acceptable in your area.

In a saddle beam deck, the beam is attached directly on top of the posts. Metal fasteners, called post-saddles, are used to align and strengthen the beam-to-post connection. The advantage is that the post bears the weight of the deck.

A notched-post deck requires 6 × 6 posts notched at the post top to accommodate the full size of the beam. The deck's weight is transferred to the posts, as in a post-and-beam deck.

In years past, a third style of beam construction, called sandwiching, was also generally acceptable for deck construction. It consisted of two beams that straddled both sides of the post, connected by long through bolts. Because this method has less strength than the saddle or notched styles, it is no longer approved by most building codes.

Tools & Materials

Tape measure
Pencil
Circular saw
Paint brush
Combination square
Screwgun
Drill
⅜" auger bit
1" spade bit
Ratchet wrench
Caulk gun
Reciprocating saw or handsaw
Pressure-treated lumber
Clear sealer-preservative
2½" galvanized deck screws
10d joist hanger nails
⅜ × 8" carriage bolts with washers and nuts
⅜ × 2" lag screws
Silicone caulk

Deck beams, resting in a notch on the tops of the posts and secured with through bolts and nuts, guarantee strong connections that will bear the weight of your deck.

How to Fabricate a Beam

Select two straight boards of the same dimension (generally 2 × 8 or larger) and lay them face to face to see which alignment comes closest to flush on all sides. Apply exterior grade construction adhesive to one board and lay the mating board onto it. Drive a pair of 10d nails near the end of the assembly to pin the boards together.

Clamp the beam members together every two or three feet, forcing the boards into alignment as you go, if necessary. Drive 10d nails in a regular, staggered pattern every 12" to 16" or so. Flip the beam over and repeat the nailing pattern from the other side.

How to Mark Post Locations on a Beam

Measure along the beam to the post locations, making sure the ends of the boards of a doubled beam are flush. Mark both the near and far edges of the post onto the beam.

Use a combination square or speed square to transfer the post marks onto the top and then the other face of the beam, allowing you to make sure the post and post hardware align with both faces.

How to Install a Beam with a Post Saddle

1

Cut the post to final height after securing it in place. Make two passes with a circular saw or one pass with a reciprocating saw. For most DIYers, the circular saw option will yield a more even cut.

2

Attach the saddle hardware to the top of the post using joist hanger screws, 10d galvanized common nails, or joist hanger nails. You must drive a fastener at every predrilled hole in the saddle hardware.

3

Set the beam into the saddle, making sure the sides of the saddle align with the layout marks on the beam.

4

Secure the beam into the saddle by driving galvanized common nails or joist hanger screws through the predrilled holes in the top half of the saddle.

How to Install a Beam for a Notched-post Deck

Remove 6 × 6 posts from post anchors and cut to finished height. Measure and mark a notch at the top of each post, sized to fit the thickness and width of the beam. Trace the lines on all sides using a framing square.

Use a circular saw to rough-cut the notches, then switch to a reciprocating saw or hand saw to finish. Reattach posts to the post anchors, with the notch-side facing away from the deck.

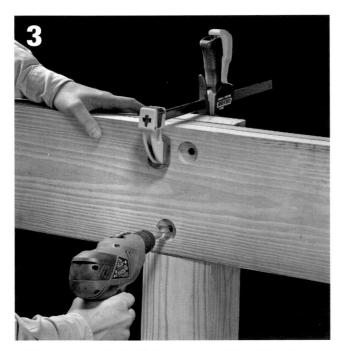

With someone's help, lift beam (crown side up) into the notches. Align beam and clamp to posts. Counterbore two ½"-deep holes, using a 1" spade bit, then drill ⅜" pilot holes through the beam and post, using a ⅜" auger bit.

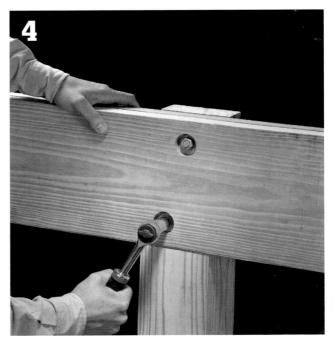

Insert carriage bolts to each pilot hole. Add a washer and nut to the counterbore-side of each, and tighten using a ratchet. Seal both ends with silicone caulk. Apply self-sealing membrane to top surfaces of beam and posts if necessary.

6. Hanging Joists

Joists provide support for the decking boards. They are attached to the ledger and header joist with galvanized metal joist hangers and are nailed to the top of the beam.

For strength and durability, use pressure-treated lumber for all joists. The exposed outside joists and header joist can be faced with redwood or cedar boards for a more attractive appearance.

Tools & Materials

Tape measure
Pencil
Hammer
Combination square
Circular saw
Paintbrush

Drill
Twist bits ($\frac{1}{16}$", $\frac{1}{4}$")
1" spade bit
Pressure-treated lumber
10d joist hanger nails

10d and 16d galvanized common nails
Clear sealer-preservative
Joist angle brackets

Galvanized metal joist hangers
$\frac{3}{8} \times 4$" lag screws and 1" washers

Metal joist hangers attached to rim joists or ledgers are practically foolproof for hanging intermediate deck joists. Look for hanger hardware that is triple-dipped galvanized metal.

How to Hang Joists

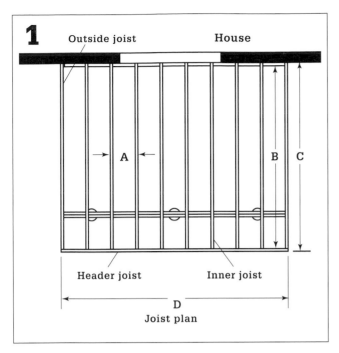

Use your deck plan to find the spacing (A) between joists, and the length of inner joists (B), outside joists (C), and header joist (D). Measure and mark lumber for outside joists, using a combination square as a guide. Cut joists with a circular saw. Seal cut ends with clear sealer-preservative.

Attach joist hanger hardware near each end of the ledger board, according to your layout. Previous building codes allowed you to face nail the joists into the ends of the ledger, but this is no longer accepted practice. Attach only enough fasteners to hold the hanger in position while you square up the joist layout.

Attach the outside joists to the top of the beam by toenailing them with 10d galvanized common nails.

Trim off the ends of structural lumber to get a clean straight edge.

(continued)

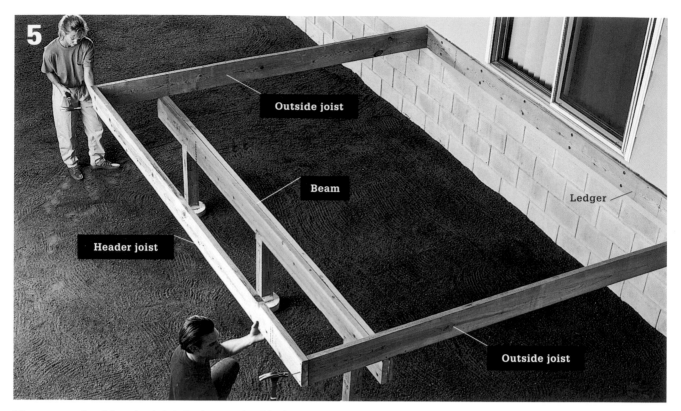

5

Outside joist

Beam

Ledger

Header joist

Outside joist

Measure and cut header joist. Seal cut ends with clear sealer-preservative. Drill 1/16" pilot holes at each end of header joist. Attach header to ends of outside joists with 16d galvanized common nails. For extra reinforcement, you can add metal corner brackets to the inside corner joints.

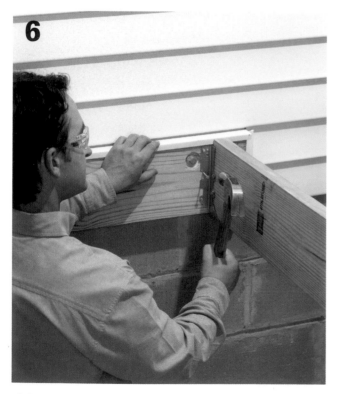

6

Finish nailing the end joist hangers, making sure you have a joist hanger nail in every punched hole in the hanger.

7

Measure along ledger from edge of outside joist, and mark where joists will be attached to ledger.

Draw the outline of each joist on the ledger, using a combination square as a guide.

Measure along the beam from outside joist, and mark where joists will cross the beam. Draw the outlines across top of both beam boards.

Measure along the header joist from the outside joist, and mark where joists will be attached to header joist. Draw the outlines on the inside of the header, using a combination square as a guide.

Attach joist hangers to the ledger and to the header joist. Position each hanger so that one of the flanges is against the joist outline. Nail one flange to framing members with 10d galvanized common nails.

(continued)

12

Cut a scrap board to use as a spacer. Hold spacer inside each joist hanger, then close the hanger around the spacer.

13

Nail the remaining side flange to the framing member with 10d joist hanger nails. Remove spacer.

14

Measure and mark lumber for joists, using a combination square as a guide. Cut joists with a circular saw or power miter saw.

15

Seal cut ends with clear sealer-preservative. Place joists in hangers with crowned edge up.

Attach the ledger joist hangers to the joists with joist hanger nails. Drive nails into both sides of each joist.

Align the joists with the outlines drawn on the top of the beam. Anchor the joists to the beam by toenailing from both sides with 10d galvanized nails.

Alternate Method

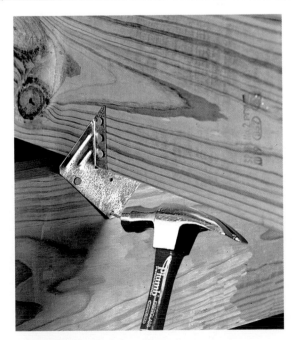

Fasten joists to beams using H-fit joist ties for strength and durability.

Attach the joists to the hangers on the joist with 10d joist hanger nails. Drive nails into both sides of each joist.

7. Laying Decking

Buy decking boards that are long enough to span the width of the deck, if possible. If boards must be butted end-to-end, make sure to stagger the joints so they do not overlap from row to row. Predrill the ends of boards to prevent screws or nails from splitting the wood.

Install decking so that there is a ⅛" gap between boards to provide drainage. Boards naturally "cup" as they age. Lay boards with the bark side facing down, so that the cupped surface cannot hold standing water.

General installation instructions for decking materials are shown here. Always follow the installation methods recommended by the manufacturer of the product you select.

Tools & Materials

Tape measure
Circular saw
Screwgun
Hammer
Drill
⅛" twist bit
Pry bar
Chalk line

Jigsaw or handsaw
Decking boards
2½" corrosion-resistant
   deck screws
Galvanized common
   nails (8d, 10d)
Redwood or cedar
   facing boards

How to Lay Decking

Position the first row of decking flush against the house. First decking board should be perfectly straight, and should be precut to proper length. Attach the first decking board by driving a pair of 2½" corrosion-resistant deck screws into each joist.

Position remaining decking boards so that ends overhang outside joists. Space boards about ⅛" apart. Attach boards to each joist with a pair of 2½" deck screws driven into each joist.

Alternate method: Attach decking boards with 10d galvanized common nails. Angle the nails toward each other to improve holding power.

3

If boards are bowed, use a pry bar to maneuver them into position while fastening.

4

Drill ⅛" pilot holes in ends of boards before attaching them to outside joists. Pilot holes prevent screws from splitting decking boards at ends.

5

After every few rows of decking are installed, measure from edge of the decking board to edge of header joist. If measurements show that the last board will not fit flush against the edge of the deck, adjust board spacing.

6

Adjust board spacing by changing the gaps between boards by a small amount over three or four rows of boards. Very small spacing changes will not be obvious to the eye.

(continued)

7

Use a chalk line to mark the edge of decking flush with the outside of deck. Cut off decking, using a circular saw. Set saw blade ⅛" deeper than thickness of decking so that saw will not cut side of deck. At areas where circular saw cannot reach, finish cutoff with a jigsaw or handsaw.

8

For a more attractive appearance, face the deck with redwood or cedar facing boards. Miter cut corners, and attach boards with deck screws or 8d galvanized nails.

Alternate facing technique: Attach facing boards so that edges of decking overhang facing.

Composite Decking

Lay composite decking as you would wood decking (pages 40 to 41). Position with the factory crown up so water will run off, and space rows ⅛" to ¼" apart for drainage.

Predrill pilot holes at ¾ the diameter of the fasteners, but do not countersink. Composite materials allow fasteners to set themselves. Use spiral shank nails, hot-dipped galvanized ceramic coated screws, or stainless steel nails or deck screws.

Cut away for clarity

Alternate method: Attach composite decking with self-tapping composite screws. These specially designed screws require no pilot holes. If the decking "mushrooms" over the screw head, use a hammer to tap back in place.

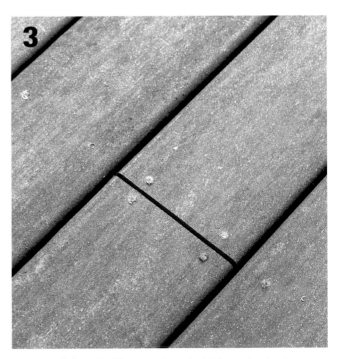

Lay remaining decking. For boards 16-ft. or shorter, leave a gap at deck ends and any butt joints, ¹⁄₁₆" for every 20°F difference between the temperature at the time of installation and the expected high temperature for the year.

Tongue-and-groove Decking

1

Position starter strip at far end of deck. Make sure it is straight and properly aligned. Attach with 2½" galvanized deck screws driven into the lower runner found under the lip of the starter strip.

2

Fit tongue of a deck board into groove of starter strip. There will be approximately a ¼" gap between the deck board and the starter strip. Fasten the deck board to the joists with 2½" galvanized deck screws, working from the middle out to the sides of the deck.

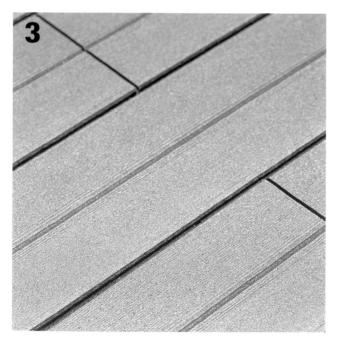

3

Continue to add decking. To lay deck boards end-to-end, leave a ⅛" gap between them, and make sure any butt joints are centered over a joist.

4

Place final deck board and attach with 2½" galvanized deck screws driven through top of the deck board into the joist. If necessary, rip final board to size, then support the board with a length of 1 × 1 and attach both to the joist. Attach facing boards to conceal exposed ends (photo 4, next page).

T-clip Decking

1

Insert 2" galvanized deck screws into T-clips. Loosely attach one T-clip to the ledger at each joist location.

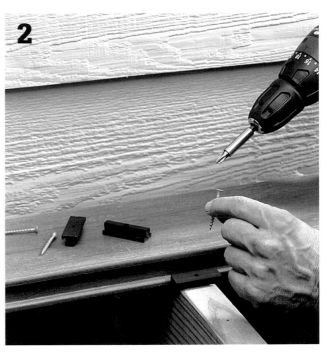

2

Position a deck board tight against the T-clips. Loosely attach T-clips against bottom lip on front side of deck board, just tight enough to keep the board in place. Fully tighten T-clips at back of board, against the house.

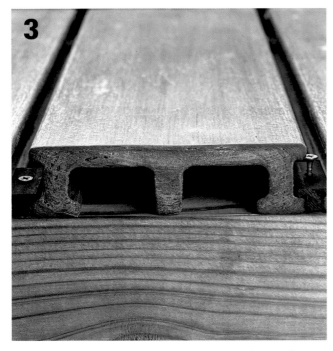

3

Push another deck board tightly against the front T-clips, attach T-clips at front of the new board, then fully tighten the previous set of T-clips. Add another deck board and repeat the process, to the end of the deck.

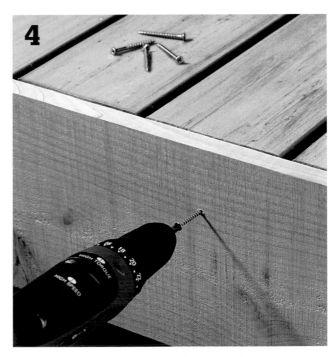

4

Cover exposed deck board ends. Miter cut corners of the facing, and drill pilot holes ¾ the diameter of the screws. Attach with 3" galvanized deck screws.

How to Install Decking with Spiked Clips

Drive a spiked clip into the edge of wood decking at joist locations. Use the included fastening block to prevent damage to the spikes.

Drive a deck screw through the hole in the clip and down at an angle through the deck board and into the joist. One screw secures two deck boards at each joist location.

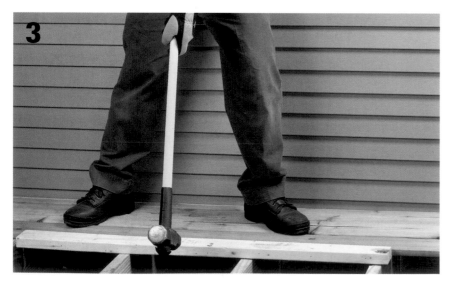

Set the adjacent deck board into place. Tap it against the clips to seat the spikes, using a scrap block and hand maul or sledge hammer.

How to Install Decking with Biscuit-style Clips

Cut a #20 biscuit slot into the edge of deck boards at each joist location using a biscuit joiner (plate joiner). Set the slot height so the bottom edge of the biscuit clip will touch the joist edge.

Insert the biscuit clip into the slot. Drive a deck screw through the hole in the clip and down at an angle through the deck board and into the joist. One screw secures two deck boards at this joist location.

Second board

#20 biscuit slots

First board

Lay a bead of construction adhesive along the edge of the joist to keep it from squeaking later. Cut slots in the adjacent deck board and fit it over the clips of the previous board.

Tip

The hidden fastener options shown here are excellent alternatives to conventional face-nailing or screwing methods. The biggest advantage is probably aesthetic: you don't have to see row after row of fastener heads any longer with these new installation products. But there are other benefits to hidden fasteners as well. Face-screwed wood decking is more prone to rotting if water collects in the screw head pockets. If you nail the decking down, the nail heads can pop up as wood decking dries and contracts or moves. Hidden fasteners eliminate both of these problems.

If you use spike- or biscuit-style clip systems, be aware that you may need to remove large sections of deck boards in order to replace a damaged or defective board in the future, because the fasteners lock adjacent boards together and hide access to the fasteners.

How to Install Decking with Undermount Deck Brackets

Install the deck brackets along the top edge of each joist, alternating brackets from one side of the joist to the other in a continuous series. Secure the brackets with screws driven into the side of the joist.

Secure the deck boards by driving screws up through the bracket holes and into the joists. Depending on space constraints, these screws can be driven from above if necessary.

Continue installing all of the deck boards from below. When you reach the last board, you may need to install it from above for access reasons. Drive deck screws through the deck board and into the joists below. To maintain the hidden fastener appearance, counterbore the pilot holes for the screws and fill the counterbore with a plug cut from a piece of scrap decking.

How to Install Decking with Undermount Clips

Set a deck board into place on the joists, and slide a clip against it so the spacer tab touches the edge of the deck board. Drive a screw through the center hole of the clip and into the joist.

Drive a deck screw up through the plastic clip and into the deck board to secure it.

Position the next deck board against the clip's spacer tab, and drive a deck screw up through the clip to fasten it in place. One clip secures two deck boards at each joist location.

8. Building Stairs

Designing deck stairs requires four calculations: **The number of steps** depends on the vertical drop of the deck. The vertical drop is the distance from the surface of the deck to the ground.

Rise is the vertical space between treads. Building codes require that the rise measurement be about 8".

Run is the depth of the treads. A convenient way to build deck stairs is to use a pair of 2 × 6s for each tread.

Span is figured by multiplying the run by the number of treads. The span lets you locate the end of the stairway, and position support posts.

Tools & Materials

Tape measure
Pencil
Framing square
Level
Plumb bob
Clamshell posthole digger
Wheelbarrow
Hoe
Circular saw
Hammer
Drill
⅛" twist bit
1" spade bit
Ratchet wrench
Caulk gun
Sand
Portland cement
Gravel
J-bolts
Metal post anchors
2 × 12 lumber
Metal cleats
¼" × 1¼" lag screws
Joist angle brackets
10d joist hanger nails
⅜" × 4" lag screws and 1" washers
2 × 6 lumber
16d galvanized common nails
Silicone caulk
Long, straight 2 × 4
Pointed stakes
Masking tape

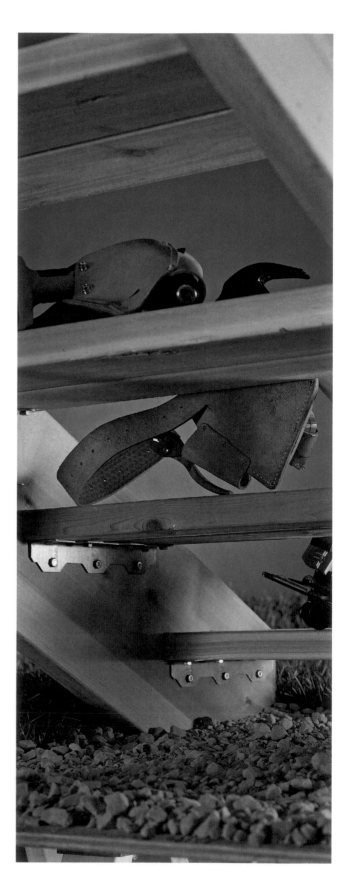

Materials for Deck Stairs

Most local building codes require that you use pressure-treated lumber for stairway posts and stringers. Install stair treads and risers cut from material that matches the surface decking. If possible, create treads that use the same board pattern as the decking. You may cover visible pressure-treated portions of the stairway with material matching the decking, too, or stain them to match the decking as closely as possible. Local codes may require handrails on stairways with three or more treads.

Platform steps feature wide treads. Each step is built on a framework of posts and joists.

Stairway Styles

Open steps have metal cleats that hold the treads between the stringers. The treads on this stairway are built with 2 × 6s to match the surface decking.

Boxed steps, built with notched stringers and solid risers, give a finished look to a deck stairway. Predrill ends of treads to prevent splitting.

Long stairways sometimes require landings. A landing is a small platform to which both flights of stairs are attached (see pages 58 to 67).

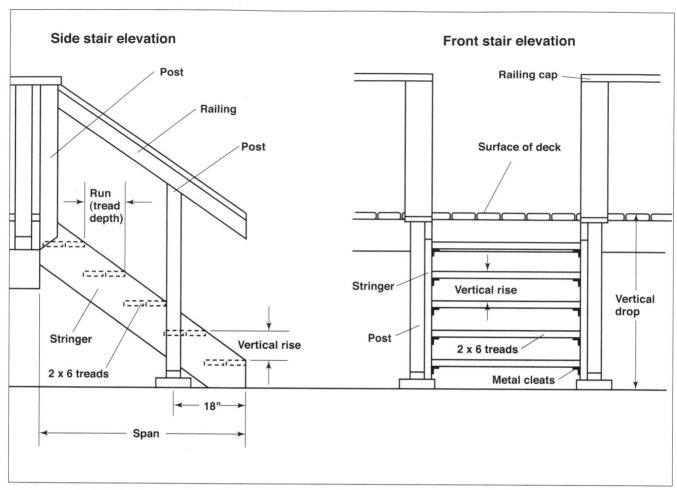

Side stair elevation

Post

Railing

Post

Run (tread depth)

Stringer

2 x 6 treads

Vertical rise

18"

Span

Front stair elevation

Railing cap

Surface of deck

Stringer

Vertical rise

Post

2 x 6 treads

Metal cleats

Vertical drop

A common deck stairway is made from two 2 × 12 stringers and pairs of 2 × 6 treads attached with metal cleats. Posts set 18" back from the end of the stairway help to anchor the stringers and the railings. Calculations needed to build stairs include the number of steps, the rise of each step, the run of each step, and the stairway span.

How to Find Measurements for Stairway Layout

			SAMPLE MEASUREMENTS (39" High Deck)
1.	Find the number of steps: Measure vertical drop from deck surface to ground. Divide by 7. Round off to nearest whole number.	Vertical drop:	39"
		÷ 7 =	÷ 5.57"
		Number of steps: =	= 6
2.	Find step rise: Divide the vertical drop by the number of steps.	Vertical drop: =	39"
		Number of steps: ÷	÷ 6
		Rise: =	= 6.5"
3.	Find step run: Typical treads made from two 2 × 6s have a run of 11¼". If your design is different, find run by measuring depth of tread, including any space between boards.	Run:	11¼"
4.	Find stairway span: Multiply the run by the number of treads. (Number of treads is always one less than number of steps.)	Run:	11¼"
		Number of treads:	× 5
		Span: =	= 56¼"

Simple Stairs: How to Build a Box-frame Step

Construct a rectangular frame for the step using dimension lumber (2 × 6 lumber is standard). Join the pieces with deck screws. The step must be at least 36" wide and 10" deep. Cut cross blocks and install them inside the frame, spaced every 16".

Dig a flat-bottomed trench, about 4" deep, where the step will rest. Fill the trench with compactible gravel, and pack with a tamper. Set the step in position, then measure and attach deck boards to form the tread of the step.

Simple Stairs: How to Build a Suspended Step

Screw 2 × 4 furring strips against one side of the deck joists where the step joists will be installed. These strips provide an offset so the step joists will not conflict with the joist hangers attached to the beam. Use a reciprocating saw and chisel to make 1½"-wide notches in the rim joist adjacent to the furring strips. *Note: To maintain adequate structural strength, notches in the joists should be no more than 1½" deep.*

Measure and cut step joists, allowing about 3 ft. of nailing surface inside the deck frame, and 10" or more of exposed tread. Make sure the step joists are level with one another, then attach them to the deck joists, using deck screws. Cut and attach deck boards to the tread area of the step.

How to Build Basic Deck Stairs

Use the stairway elevation drawings to find measurements for stair stringers and posts. Use a pencil and framing square to outline where stair stringers will be attached to the side of the deck.

Locate the post footings so they are 18" back from the end of stairway span. Lay a straight 2 × 4 on the deck so that it is level and square to side of deck. Use a plumb bob to mark the ground at centerpoints of footings.

Dig holes and pour footings for posts. Attach metal post anchors to footings and install posts. Check with your building department to find out if 6 × 6 posts are now required.

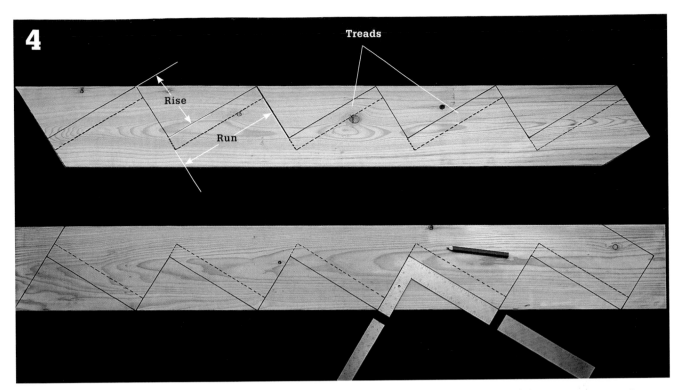

4

Treads

Rise

Run

Lay out stair stringers. Use tape to mark the rise measurement on one leg of a framing square, and the run measurement on the other leg. Beginning at one end of stringer, position the square with tape marks flush to edge of board, and outline the rise and run for each step. Then draw in the tread outline against the bottom of each run line. Use a circular saw to trim ends of stringers as shown.

5

Attach metal tread cleats flush with bottom of each tread outline, using ¼" × 1¼" lag screws. Drill ⅛" pilot holes to prevent the screws from splitting the wood.

6

Attach angle brackets to upper ends of stringers, using 10d joist hanger nails. Brackets should be flush with cut ends of stringers.

(continued)

7

Position the stair stringers against side of deck, over the stringer outlines. Align top point of stringer flush with the surface of the deck. Attach stringers by nailing the angle brackets to the deck with 10d joist hanger nails.

8

Drill two ¼" pilot holes through each stringer and into each adjacent post. Counterbore each hole to depth of ½", using a 1" spade bit. Attach stringers to posts with ⅜" × 4" lag screws and washers, using a ratchet wrench or impact driver. Seal screw heads with silicone caulk.

9

Measure width of stair treads. Cut two 2 × 6s for each tread, using a circular saw.

10

For each step, position the front 2 × 6 on the tread cleat, so that the front edge is flush with the tread outline on the stringers.

Drill ⅛" pilot holes, then attach the front 2 × 6 to the cleats with ¼" × 1¼" lag screws.

Position the rear 2 × 6 on the cleats, allowing a small space between boards. Use a 16d nail as a spacing guide. Drill ⅛" pilot holes, and attach 2 × 6 to cleats with ¼" × 1¼" lag screws. Repeat for remaining steps.

Stair Variation

Notched stringers precut from pressure-treated wood are available at building centers. Edges of cutout areas should be coated with sealer-preservative to prevent rot.

9. Building Stairs with Landings

Designing and building a stairway with a landing can be one of the most challenging elements of a deck project. Precision is crucial, since building codes have very exact standards for stairway construction. To ensure that the steps for both the top and bottom staircases have the same vertical rise and tread depth, the landing must be set at the right position and height.

Even for professional builders, designing a stairway layout is a process of trial and revision. Begin by creating a preliminary layout that fits your situation, but as you plan and diagram the project, be prepared to revise the layout to satisfy code requirements and the demands of your building site. Measure your site carefully, and work out all the details on paper before you begin any work. Accuracy and meticulous planning will help ensure that your steps are level and uniform in size.

Remember that local building codes may require handrails for any stairway with three or more risers.

Stairway Basics

The goal of any stairway is to allow people to move easily and safely from one level to another. When designing a deck stairway, the builder must consider the vertical drop—the vertical distance from the surface of the deck to the ending point; and the span—the horizontal distance from the starting point to the end of the stairway.

During the planning stage, the vertical drop is divided into a series of equal-size steps, called rises. Similarly, the horizontal span is divided into a series of equal-size runs. On a stairway with a landing, there are two span measurements to consider: the distance from the deck to the edge of the landing, and from the landing to the end point on the ground. In general, the combined horizontal span of the staircases, not counting the landing, should be 40% to 60% more than the total vertical drop.

For safety and comfort, the components of a stairway must be built according to clearly prescribed guidelines, as listed on page 59.

A landing functions essentially as a large step that interrupts a tall stairway. For the builder, the landing provides a convenient spot from which to change the direction of the stairway. For the homeowner, the landing provides a spot to catch your breath momentarily while climbing.

Anatomy of a Stair with Landing

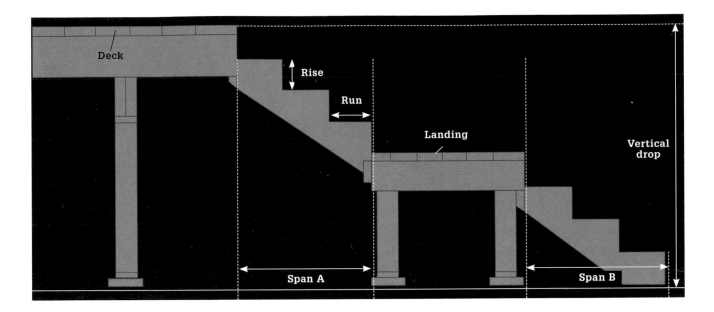

The challenge when planning a stairway is adjusting the preliminary layout and the step dimensions as needed to ensure that the stairway fits the building site and is comfortable to use.

Rises must be no less than 4" and no more than 8" high.

Runs, the horizontal depth of each step, must be at least 10". The number of runs in a staircase is always one less than the number of rises.

Combined sum of the step rise and run should be about 18" to 20". Steps built to this guideline are the most comfortable to use.

Variation between the largest and smallest rise or run measurement can be no more than ⅜".

Stair width must be at least 36", so two people can comfortably pass one another.

Stringers should be spaced no more than 36" apart. For added support, a center stringer is recommended for any staircase with more than three steps.

Landings serve as oversized steps; their height must be set as precisely as the risers for the other steps in the stairway. Landings should be at least 36" square, or as wide as the staircase itself. U-shaped stairways should have oversized landings, at least 1 ft. wider than the combined width of the two staircases. Landings very often require reinforcement with diagonal cross braces between the support posts.

Concrete footings should support all stringers resting on the ground.

Code Update: Stair Pads

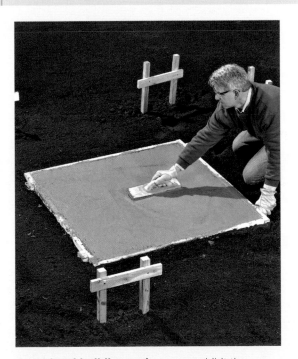

Some local building codes now prohibit the use of a concrete stair pad to support the bottom run of stair stringers. The "floating" nature of a slab like this allows it to move up and down as the ground freezes and thaws, and that causes the stairs to shift as well. Use full-depth concrete footings instead of a pad to support your deck stairs (see page 66).

Construction Details

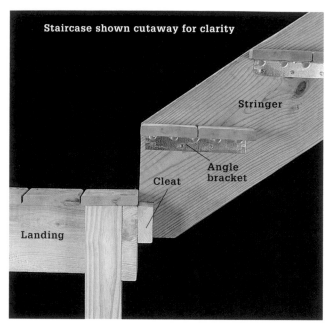

Stringers for the top staircase rest on a 2 × 4 cleat attached to the side of the landing. The stringers are notched to fit around the cleat. On the outside stringers, angle brackets support the treads.

Steps may be boxed in the riser boards, and may have treads that overhang the front edge of the step for a more finished look. Treads should overhang the riser boards by no more than 1".

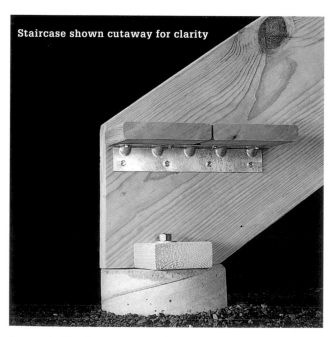

Concrete footings support the stringers for the lower staircase. J-bolts are inserted into the footings while the concrete is still wet. After the footings dry, wooden cleats are attached to the bolts to create surfaces for anchoring the stringers. After the staircase is positioned, the stringers are nailed or screwed to the cleats.

Center stringers are recommended for any staircase that has more than 3 steps or is more than 36" wide. Center stringers are supported by a 2 × 6 nailer attached with metal straps to the bottom of the rim joist. The bottom edge of the nailer is beveled to match the angle of the stringers. The center stringer is attached by driving deck screws through the back of the nailer and into the stringer.

How to Create a Preliminary Layout

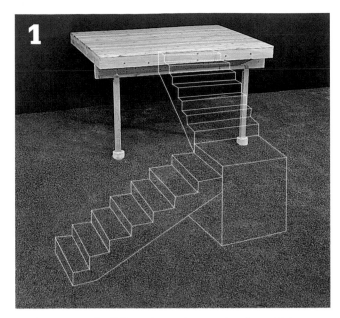

Evaluate your building site and try to visualize which stairway design best fits your needs. When creating a preliminary layout, it is generally best to position the landing so the upper and lower staircases will be of equal length. Select a general design idea.

Establish a rough starting point for the stairway on the deck, and an ending point on the ground that conforms with your design. Mark the starting point on the rim joist, and mark the ending point with two stakes, spaced to equal the planned width of your stairway. This is a rough layout only; later calculations will give you the precise measurements.

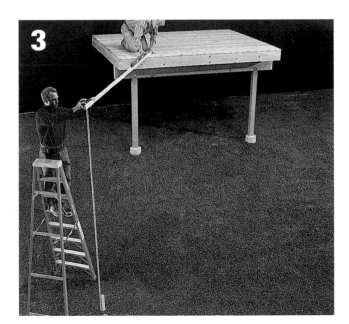

To determine the vertical drop of the stairway, extend a straight 2 × 4 from the starting point on the deck to a spot level with the deck directly over the ending point on the ground. Measure the distance to the ground; this measurement is the total vertical drop. *Note: If the ending point is more than 10 ft. from the starting point, use a mason's string and line level to establish a reference point from which to measure.*

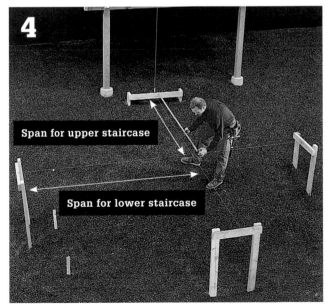

Span for upper staircase

Span for lower staircase

Measure the horizontal span for each staircase. First, use batterboards to establish level layout strings representing the edges of the staircases. Find the span for the upper staircase by measuring from a point directly below the edge of the deck out to the edge of the landing. Measure the span for the lower staircase from the landing to the endpoint.

Create Final Stair Landing Layouts

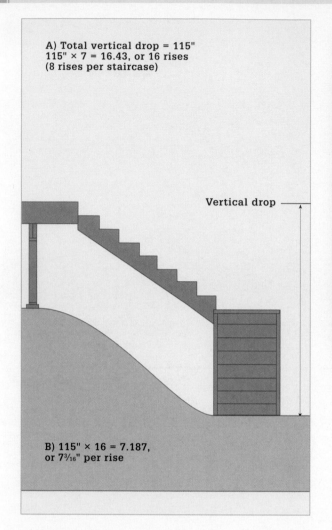

A) Total vertical drop = 115"
115" × 7 = 16.43, or 16 rises
(8 rises per staircase)

Vertical drop

B) 115" × 16 = 7.187,
or 7³⁄₁₆" per rise

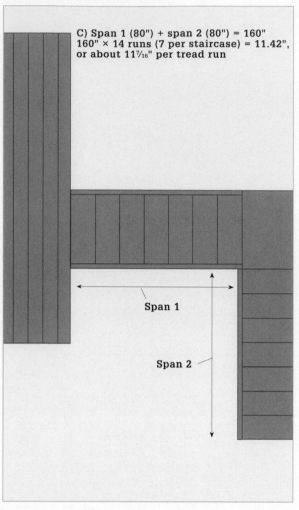

C) Span 1 (80") + span 2 (80") = 160"
160" × 14 runs (7 per staircase) = 11.42",
or about 11⁷⁄₁₆" per tread run

Span 1

Span 2

ILLUSTRATIONS ABOVE:

Find the total number of step rises you will need by dividing the vertical drop by 7, rounding off fractions. (A, example above). Next, determine the exact height for each step rise by dividing the vertical drop by the number of rises (B).

Find the horizontal run for each step by adding the spans of both staircases (not including the landing), then dividing by the number of runs (C). Remember that the number of runs in a staircase is always one less than the number of rises.

If the layout does not conform with the guidelines on page 129, adjust the stairway starting point, ending point, or landing, then recalculate the measurements. After finding all dimensions, return to your building site and adjust the layout according to your final plan.

ILLUSTRATIONS NEXT PAGE:

Lay out stringers on 2 × 12 lumber using a carpenter's square. Trim off the waste sections with a circular saw, finishing the notched cuts with a handsaw. In the illustrations on page 133, the waste sections are left unshaded. In standard deck construction, the outside stringers are fitted with metal tread supports that are attached to the inside faces of the stringers. The middle stringer in each flight of stairs is notched to create surfaces that support the stair treads—when cut, these surfaces must align with the tops of the metal tread supports. For the upper staircase stringers, notches are cut at the bottom, front edges to fit over a 2 × 4 cleat that is attached to the landing (see page 55). The top of each notch should lie below the nose of the bottom tread by a distance equal to one rise plus the thickness of a decking board (see next page).

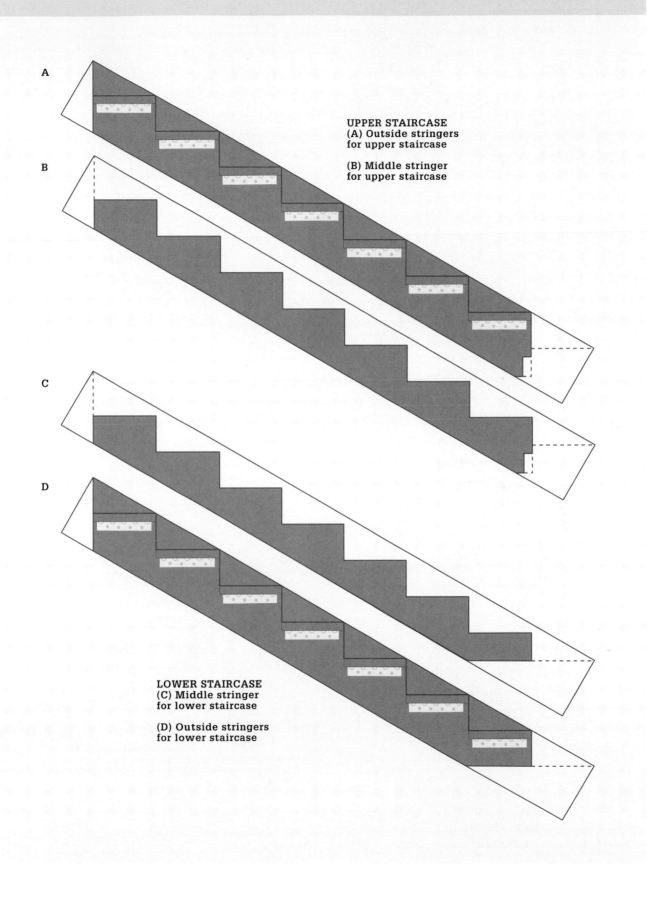

UPPER STAIRCASE
(A) Outside stringers
for upper staircase

(B) Middle stringer
for upper staircase

LOWER STAIRCASE
(C) Middle stringer
for lower staircase

(D) Outside stringers
for lower staircase

How to Build Stairs with a Landing

Begin construction by building the landing. On a flat surface, build the landing frame from 2 × 6 lumber. Join the corners with 3" deck screws, then check for square by measuring diagonals. Adjust the frame until the diagonals are equal, then tack braces across the corners to hold the frame square.

Using your plan drawing, find the exact position of the landing on the ground, then set the frame in position and adjust it for level. Drive stakes to mark locations for the landing posts, using a plumb bob as a guide. Install the footings and posts for the landing.

From the top of the deck, measure down a distance equal to the vertical drop for the upper staircase. Attach a 2 × 4 reference board across the deck posts at this height. Position a straightedge on the reference board and against the landing posts so it is level, and mark the posts at this height. Measure down a distance equal to the thickness of the decking boards, and mark reference lines to indicate where the top of the landing frame will rest.

Attach the landing frame to the posts at the reference lines. Make sure the landing is level, then secure it with joist ties attached to the posts with ⅝" × 3" lag screws. Cut off the posts flush with the top of the landing frame, using a reciprocating saw.

Remove the diagonal braces from the top of the landing frame, then cut and install joists. (For a diagonal decking pattern, space the joists every 12".) Attach the decking boards, and trim them to the edge of the frame.

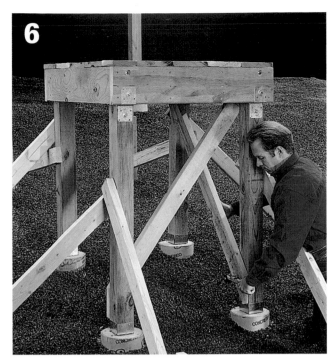

For extra support and to help prevent sway, create permanent cross braces by attaching 2 × 4 boards diagonally from the bottoms of the posts to the inside of the landing frame. Brace at least two sides of the landing. Remove the temporary braces and stakes holding the posts.

Lay out and cut all stringers for both the upper and lower staircases (page 55). For the center stringers only, cut notches where the treads will rest. Start the notches with a circular saw, then finish the cuts with a handsaw. Measure and cut all tread boards.

Use ¾"-long lag screws to attach angle brackets to the stringers where the treads will rest, then turn the stringers upside down and attach the treads with lag screws. Gaps between tread boards should be no more than ⅜".

(continued)

Dig and pour a concrete footing to support each stringer for the lower staircase. Make sure the footings are level and are the proper height in relation to the landing. Install a metal J-bolt in each footing while the concrete is wet, positioning the bolts so they will be offset about 2" from the stringers. After the concrete dries, cut 2 × 4 footing cleats, drill holes in them, and attach them to the J-bolts using nuts.

Attach a 2 × 6 nailer to the landing to support the center stringer (page 60), then set the staircase in place, making sure the outside stringers are flush with the top of the decking. Use corner brackets and joist-hanger nails to anchor the stringers to the rim joist and nailer. Attach the bottoms of the stringers by nailing them to the footing cleats.

Measure and cut a 2 × 4 cleat to match the width of the upper staircase, including the stringers. Use lag screws to attach the cleat to the rim joist on the landing, flush with the tops of the joists. Notch the bottoms of all stringers to fit around the cleat (page 60), and attach angle brackets on the stringers to support the treads.

To support the center stringer at the top of the staircase, measure and cut a 2 × 6 nailer equal to the width of the staircase. Attach the nailer to the rim joist with metal straps and screws.

Position the stringers so they rest on the landing cleat. Make sure the stringers are level and properly spaced, then toenail the bottoms of the stringers into the cleat, using galvanized 16d nails. At the top of the staircase, use angle brackets to attach the outside stringers to the rim joist and the middle stringer to the nailer.

Measure, cut, and position tread boards over the angle brackets, then attach them from below, using ¾"-long lag screws. The gap between tread boards should be no more than ⅜". After completing the stairway, install railings (pages 72 to 75).

10. Deck Railing Basics

Railings must be sturdy and firmly attached to the framing members of the deck. Never attach railing posts to the surface decking. Check local building codes for guidelines regarding railing construction. Most codes require that railings be at least 36" above decking. Vertical balusters should be spaced no more than 4" apart. In some areas, a grippable handrail may be required for any stairway over four treads. Check with your local building inspector for the building codes in your area.

Tools & Materials

Tape measure
Pencil
Power miter saw
Drill
Twist bits (⅛", ¼")
1" spade bit
Combination square
Awl
Ratchet wrench
Caulk gun
Reciprocating saw
    or circular saw
Jigsaw with wood-
    cutting blade

Level
Railing lumber
    (4 × 4s, 2 × 6s,
    2 × 4s, 2 × 2s)
Clear sealer-
    preservative
⅜ × 4" lag screws
    and 1" washers
Silicone caulk
2½" corrosion-
    resistant
    deck screws
10d galvanized
    common nails

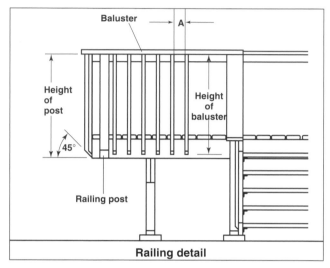

Railing detail

Refer to your deck design plan for spacing (A) and length of railing posts and balusters. Posts should be spaced no more than 6 feet apart.

Railings are mandatory safety features for any deck that's more than 30 inches above grade. There are numerous code issues and stipulations that will dictate how you build your deck railings. Consult with your local building inspector for any code clarification you may need.

Types of Railings

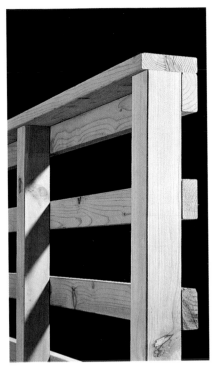

Vertical balusters with posts and rails are a good choice for houses with strong vertical lines. A vertical baluster railing like the one shown above is a good choice where children will be present.

Horizontal railings are often used on low, ranch-style homes. Horizontal railings are made of vertical posts, two or more wide horizontal rails, and a railing cap.

Lattice panels add a decorative touch to a deck. They also provide extra privacy.

Railing Codes

Railings usually are required by building code on any deck that is more than 30" high. Select a railing design that fits the style of your home.

For example, on a low, ranch-style house, choose a deck railing with wide, horizontal rails. On a Tudor-style home with a steep roof, choose a railing with closely spaced, vertical balusters. See pages 156 to 169 for information on how to build other railing styles, including a curved railing.

Some codes may require easily gripped hand rails for stairways. Check with your local building inspector.

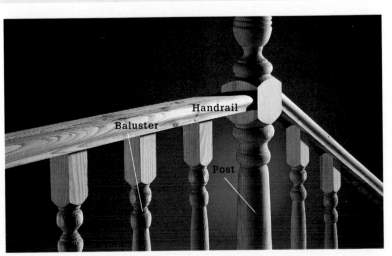

Preshaped products let you easily build decorative deck railings. Railing products include shaped handrails, balusters, and posts.

How to Install a Wood Deck Railing

Measure and cut 4 × 4 posts, using a power miter saw or circular saw. Cut off tops of the posts square, and cut the bottoms at 45° angle. Seal cut ends of lumber with clear sealer-preservative.

Measure and cut balusters for main deck, using a power miter saw or circular saw. Cut off tops of the balusters square, and cut bottoms at 45° angle. Seal cut ends of lumber with clear sealer-preservative.

Drill two ¼" pilot holes spaced 2" apart through bottom end of each post. Counterbore each pilot hole to ½" depth, using a 1" spade bit.

Drill two ⅛" pilot holes spaced 4" apart near bottom end of each baluster. Drill two ⅛" pilot holes at top of each baluster, spaced 1½" apart.

Measure and mark position of posts around the outside of the deck, using a combination square as a guide. Plan to install a post on outside edge of each stair stringer.

Position each post with beveled end flush with bottom of deck. Plumb post with a level. Insert a screwdriver or nail into pilot holes and mark side of deck.

Remove post and drill ¼" pilot holes into side of deck.

Attach railing posts to side of deck with ⅜" × 4" lag screws and washers, using a ratchet wrench or impact driver. Seal screw heads with silicone caulk.

Measure and cut 2 × 4 side rails. Position rails with edges flush to tops of posts, and attach to posts with 2½" corrosion-resistant deck screws.

(continued)

Join 2 × 4s for long rails by cutting ends at 45º angles. Drill 1/16" pilot holes to prevent nails from splitting end grain, and attach rails with 10d galvanized nails. (Screws may split mitered ends.)

Attach ends of rails to stairway posts, flush with edges of posts, as shown. Drill 1/8" pilot holes, and attach rails with 2½" deck screws.

At stairway, measure from surface of decking to the top of the upper stairway post (A).

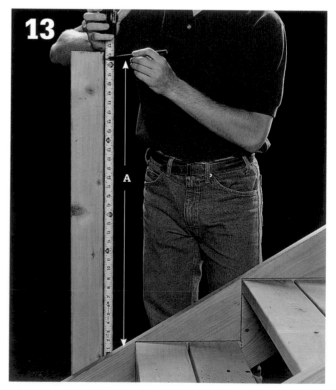

Transfer measurement A to lower stairway post, measuring from the edge of the stair stringer.

14

Rail parallel

Position 2 × 4 rail against inside of stairway posts. Align rail with top rear corner of top post and with the pencil mark on the lower post. Have a helper attach rail temporarily with 2½" deck screws.

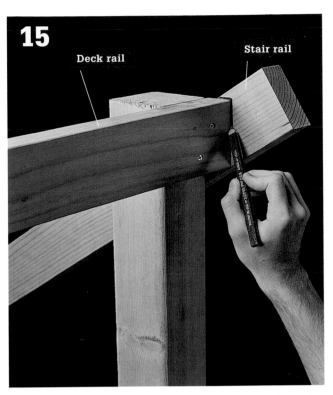

15

Deck rail

Stair rail

Mark the outline of the post and the deck rail on the back side of the stairway rail.

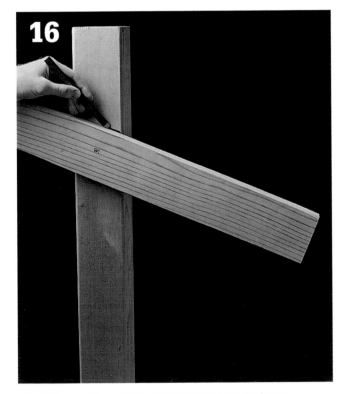

16

Mark the outline of the stairway rail on the lower stairway post.

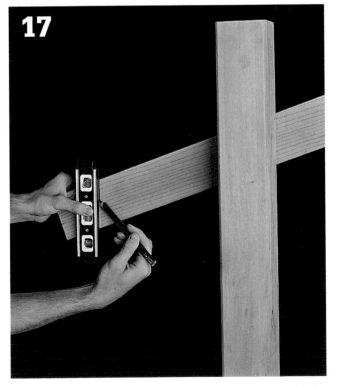

17

Use a level to mark a plumb cutoff line at the bottom end of the stairway rail. Remove the rail.

(continued)

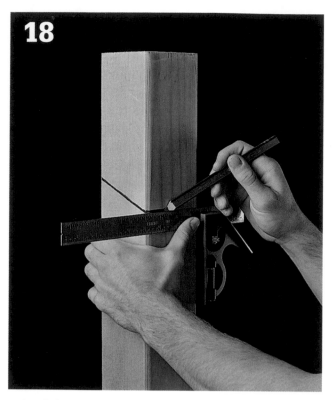

Extend the pencil lines across both sides of the stairway post, using a combination square as a guide.

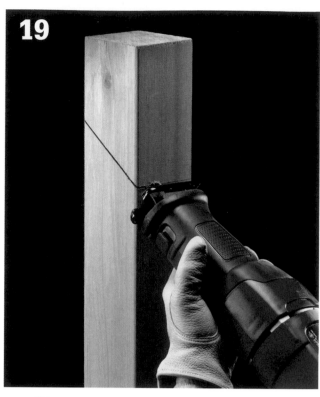

Cut off lower stairway post along diagonal cutoff line, using a reciprocating saw or circular saw.

Use a jigsaw to cut the stairway rail along the marked outlines.

Position the stairway rail flush against top edge of posts. Drill ⅛" pilot holes, then attach rail to posts with 2½" deck screws.

Use a spacer block to ensure equal spacing between balusters. Beginning next to a plumb railing post, position each baluster tight against spacer block, with top of baluster flush to top of rail. Attach each baluster with 2½" deck screws.

For stairway, position baluster against stringer and rail, and adjust for plumb. Draw diagonal cutoff line on top of baluster, using top of stair rail as a guide. Cut baluster on marked line, using power miter saw. Seal ends with clear sealer-preservative.

Beginning next to upper stairway post, position each baluster tight against spacer block, with top flush to top of stair rail. Attach baluster with 2½" deck screws.

Position 2 × 6 cap so edge is flush with inside edge of rail. Drill ⅛" pilot holes, and attach cap to rail with 2½" deck screws driven every 12". Also drive screws into each post and into every third baluster. For long caps, bevel ends at 45º. Drill ¹⁄₁₆" pilot holes, and attach at post using 10d nails.

(continued)

At corners, miter ends of railing cap at 45°. Drill ⅛" pilot holes, and attach cap to post with 2½" deck screws.

At top of stairs, cut cap so that it is flush with stairway rail. Drill ⅛" pilot holes and attach cap with 2½" deck screws.

Measure and cut cap for stairway rail. Mark outline of post on side of cap, and bevel cut the ends of the cap.

Position cap over the stairway rail and balusters so that edge of cap is flush with inside edge of rail. Drill ⅛" pilot holes, and attach cap to rail with 2½" deck screws driven every 12". Also drive screws through cap into stair post and into every third baluster.

Wood Railing Style Variations

Vertical baluster railing is a popular style because it complements most house styles. To improve the strength and appearance of the railing, the advanced variation shown here uses a "false mortise" design. The 2 × 2 balusters are mounted on 2 × 2 horizontal rails that slide into mortises notched into the posts.

Horizontal railing visually complements modern ranch-style houses with predominantly horizontal lines. For improved strength and a more attractive appearance, the style shown here features 1 × 4 rails set on edge into dadoes cut in the faces of the posts. A cap rail running over all posts and top rails helps unify and strengthen the railing.

Wall-style railing is framed with short 2 × 4 stud walls attached flush with the edges of the deck. The stud walls and rim joists are then covered with siding materials, usually chosen to match the siding on the house. A wall-style railing creates a more private space and visually draws the deck into the home, providing a unified appearance.

Stairway railings are required for any stairway with more than three steps. They are usually designed to match the style used on the deck railing.

11. Finishing a New Wood Deck

Finish a deck with clear sealer-preservative or staining sealer. Sealer-preservatives protect wood from water and rot, and are often used on cedar or redwood because they preserve the original color of the wood. If you want the wood to look weathered, wait several months before applying sealer-preservative.

Staining sealers, sometimes called toners, are often applied to pressure-treated lumber to give it the look of redwood or cedar. Staining sealers are available in a variety of colors.

For best protection, use finishing products with an alkyd base. Apply fresh finish each year.

Tools & Materials

Belt sander
Sandpaper
Shop vacuum
Pressure sprayer
Eye protection

Paint brush
Clear sealer-
   preservative or
   staining sealer

Tip

Use an orbital sander to smooth out any rough areas before applying finish to decking boards, railings, or stair treads.

A hand-pump style sprayer is inexpensive and speeds up the finish application process.

How to Finish a Redwood or Cedar Deck

Test wood surface by sprinkling water on it. If wood absorbs water quickly, it is ready to be sealed. If wood does not absorb water, let it dry for several weeks before sealing.

Sand rough areas and vacuum deck. Apply clear sealer to all wood surfaces, using a pressure sprayer. If possible, apply sealer to underside of decking and to joist, beams, and posts.

Use a paint brush to work sealer into cracks and narrow areas that could trap water.

How to Finish a Pressure-treated Deck

Sand rough areas and vacuum the deck. Apply a staining sealer (toner) to all deck wood, using a pressure sprayer.

Use a paint brush to smooth out drips and runs. Porous wood may require a second coat of staining sealer for even coverage.

12. Ground Level Walkout Deck

Here's a deck that's classic in its simplicity. Moderately sized and easy to build, this rectangular deck won't cost you an arm and a leg—in either time or money. The framing and decking plans are quite straightforward, and you can likely build the entire deck in just two or three weekends, even with limited carpentry and building experience. Within just a few weeks time, you can transform your yard into a congenial gathering place for cooking, entertaining and just plain relaxing; a place where you, your family, and your friends can enjoy the fresh air in convenience and comfort.

Extend your living space and increase your home's value.

Cutaway View

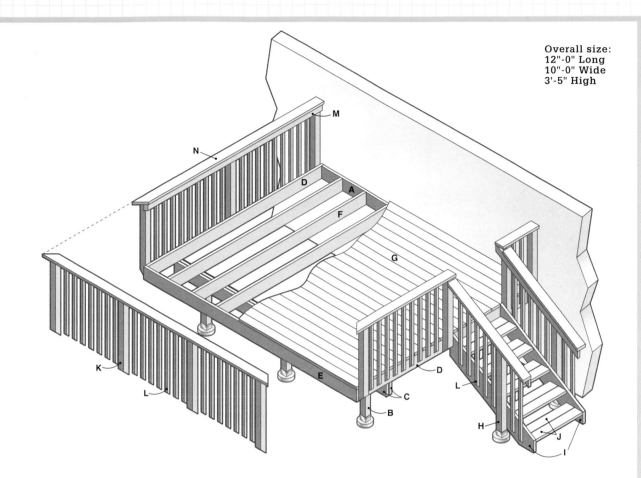

Overall size:
12"-0" Long
10"-0" Wide
3'-5" High

Supplies

10"-diameter footing forms (3)
8"-diameter footing forms (2)
J-bolts (5)
6 × 6" metal post anchors (3)
4 × 4" metal post anchors (2)
6 × 6" metal post-beam caps (3)
2 × 8" joist hangers (16)
1½ × 6" angle brackets (6)
1½ × 10" angle brackets (10)
3" galvanized deck screws
16d galvanized nails
2½" galvanized deck screws
2½" galvanized screws
⅜ × 4" lag screws and washers (20)
⅜ × 5" lag screws and washers (22)
¼ × 1¼" lag screws and washers (80)
Flashing (12 ft.)
Exterior silicone caulk (3 tubes)
Concrete as needed

Lumber List

Qty.	Size	Material	Part
4	2 × 8" × 12'	Trtd. lumber	Ledger (A), Beam bds (C), Rim joist (E)
1	6 × 6" × 8'	Trtd. lumber	Deck posts (B)
10	2 × 8" × 10'	Trtd. lumber	End joists (D), Joists (F)
25	2 × 6" × 12'	Cedar	Decking (G), Rail cap (N)
7	4 × 4" × 8'	Cedar	Stair posts (H), Rail post (K)
2	2 × 12" × 8'	Cedar	Stringers (I)
5	2 × 6" × 6'	Cedar	Treads (J)
32	2 × 2" × 8'	Cedar	Balusters (L)
2	2 × 4" × 12'	Cedar	Top rail (M)
2	2 × 4" × 10'	Cedar	Top rail (M)

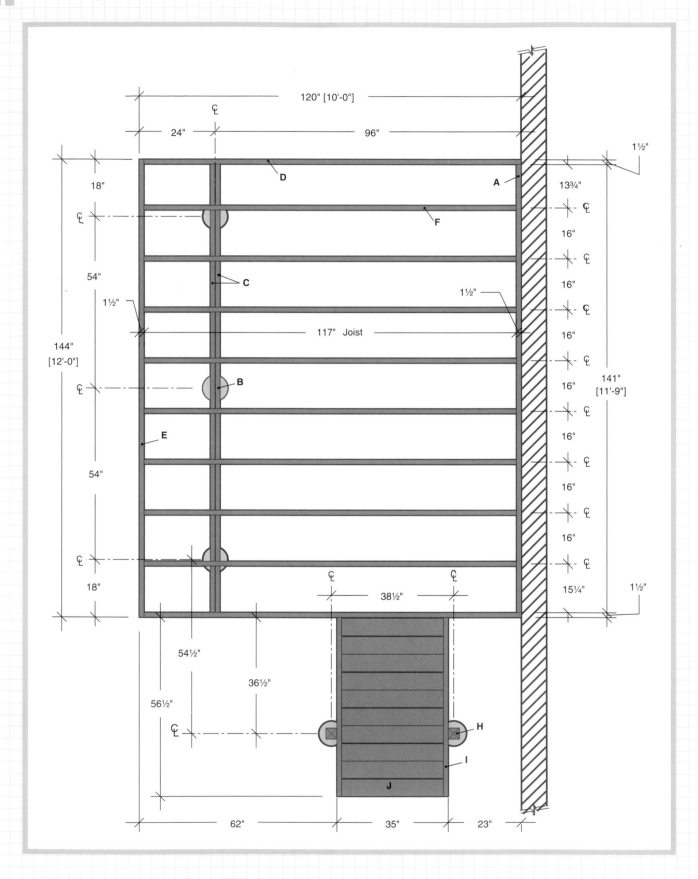

Elevation

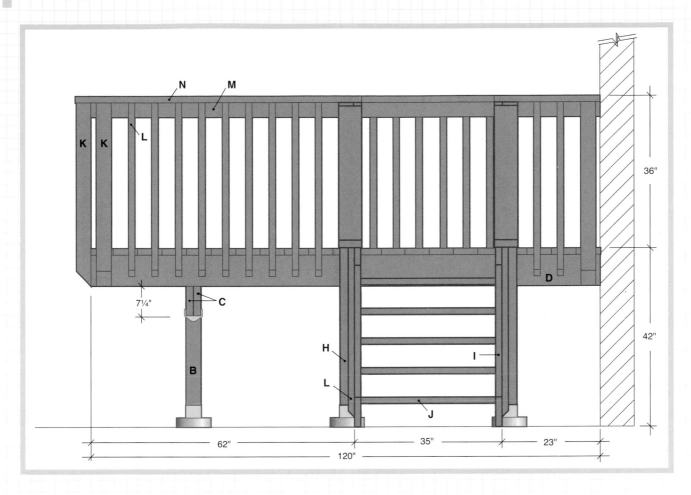

Stairway Detail

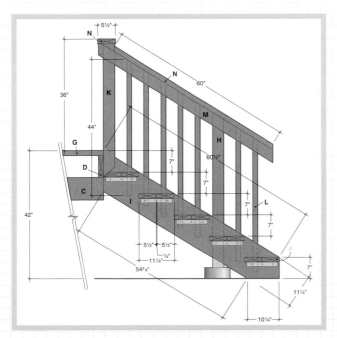

Railing Detail

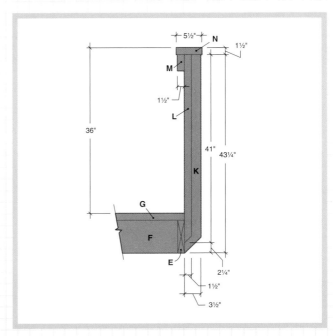

How to Build a Ground-level Walkout Deck

ATTACH THE LEDGER

Draw a level outline on the siding to show where the ledger and the end joists will fit against the house. Install the ledger so that the surface of the decking boards will be 1" below the indoor floor level. This height difference prevents rainwater or melted snow from seeping into the house.

Cut out the siding along the outline with a circular saw. To prevent the blade from cutting the sheathing that lies underneath the siding, set the blade depth to the same thickness as the siding. Finish the cutout with a chisel, holding the beveled side in to ensure a straight cut.

Cut galvanized flashing to the length of the cutout, using metal snips. Slide the flashing up under the siding at the top of the cutout.

Measure and cut the ledger (A) from pressure-treated lumber. Center the ledger end to end in the cutout, with space at each end for the end joist.

Brace the ledger in position under the flashing. Tack the ledger into place with galvanized deck screws.

Drill pairs of ¼" pilot holes at 16" intervals through the ledger and into the house header joist. Counterbore each pilot hole ½", using a 1" spade bit. Attach the ledger to the wall with ⅜ × 4" lag screws and washers, using a ratchet wrench.

Apply a thick bead of silicone caulk between siding and flashing. Also seal the lag screw heads and the cracks at the ends of the ledger.

POUR THE FOOTINGS

Referring to the measurements shown in the Framing Plan, page 82, mark the centerlines of the two outer footings on the ledger and drive nails at these locations.

Set up temporary batterboards and stretch a mason's string out from the ledger at each location. Make sure the strings are perpendicular to the ledger, and measure along the strings to find the centerpoints of the posts.

Set up additional batterboards and stretch another string parallel to the ledger across the post centerpoints.

Check the mason's strings for square, by measuring diagonally from corner to corner and adjusting the strings so that the measurements are equal.

Measure along the cross string and mark the center post location with a piece of tape.

Use a plumb bob to transfer the footing centerpoints to the ground, and drive a stake to mark each point.

Remove the mason's strings and dig the post footings, using a clamshell digger or power auger. Pour 2" to 3" of loose gravel into each hole for drainage. *Note: When measuring the footing size and depth, make sure you comply with your local building code, which may require flaring the base.*

Cut the footing forms to length, using a reciprocating saw or handsaw, and insert them into the footing holes, leaving 2" above ground level. Pack soil around the forms for support, and fill the forms with concrete, tamping with a long stick or rod to eliminate any air pockets.

Screed the tops flush with a straight 2 × 4. Insert a J-bolt into each footing, set so ¾" to 1" of thread is exposed. Retie the mason's strings and position the J-bolts at the exact center of the posts, using a plumb bob as a guide. Clean the bolt threads before concrete sets.

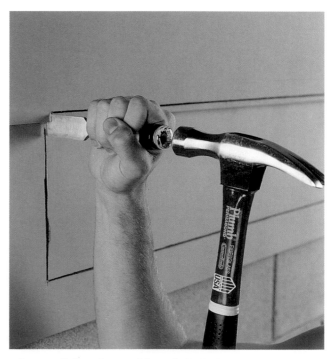

After outlining the position of the ledger and cutting the siding with a circular saw, use a chisel to finish the corners of the cutout.

After the posts have been set in place and braced plumb, use a straight 2 × 4 and a level to mark the top of the beam on each post.

SET THE POSTS

Lay a long, straight 2 × 4 flat across the footings, parallel to the ledger. With one edge tight against the J-bolts, draw a reference line across each footing.

Place a metal post anchor on each footing, centering it over the J-bolt and squaring it with the reference line. Attach the post anchors by threading a nut over each bolt and tightening with a ratchet wrench.

Cut the posts to length, adding approximately 6" for final trimming. Place the posts in the anchors and tack into place with one nail.

With a level as a guide, use braces and stakes to plumb the posts. Finish nailing the posts to the anchors.

Determine the height of the beam by extending a straight 2 × 4 from the bottom edge of the ledger across the face of a post. Level the 2 × 4, and draw a line on the post.

From that line, measure 7¼" down the post and mark the bottom of the beam. Using a level, transfer this line to the remaining posts.

Use a combination square to extend the level line completely around each post. Cut the posts to this finished height, using a reciprocating saw or hand saw.

INSTALL THE BEAM

Cut the beam boards (C) several inches longer than necessary, to allow for final trimming.

Join the beam boards together with 2½" galvanized deck screws. Mark the post locations on the top edges and sides, using a combination square as a guide.

Attach the post-beam caps to the tops of the posts. Position the caps on the post tops, and attach using 10d joist hanger nails.

Lift the beam into the post-beam caps, with the crown up. Align the post reference lines on the beam with the post-beam caps. *Note: You should have at least two helpers when installing boards of this size and length, at this height.*

Fasten the post-beam caps to the beam on both sides using 10d joist hanger nails.

INSTALL THE FRAME

Measure and cut the end joists to length using a circular saw.

Attach end joists to the ends of the ledger with 10d common nails.

Measure and cut the rim joist (E) to length with a circular saw. Fasten to end joists with 16d galvanized nails.

Square up the frame by measuring corner to corner and adjusting until measurements are equal. Toenail the end joists in place on top of the beam, and trim the beam to length.

Reinforce each inside corner of the frame with an angle bracket fastened with 10d joist hanger nails.

Install joists in hangers with crown side up.

(continued)

To locate the stairway footings, refer to the measurements in the Framing Plan, and extend a straight 2 × 4 perpendicularly from the deck. Use a plumb bob to transfer centerpoints to the ground.

INSTALL THE JOISTS

Mark the outlines of the inner joists (F) on the ledger, beam, and rim joist (see Framing Plan, page 82), using a tape measure and a combination square.

Attach joist hangers to the ledger and rim joist with 10d joist hanger nails, using a scrap 2 × 8 as a spacer to achieve the correct spread for each hanger.

Measure, mark and cut lumber for inner joists, using a circular saw. Place the joists in the hangers with crown side up, and attach at both ends with 10d joist hanger nails. Be sure to use all the holes in the hangers.

Align the joists with the marks on top of the beam, and toenail in place.

LAY THE DECKING

Cut the first decking board (G) to length, position it against the house, and attach by driving a pair of 2½" galvanized deck screws into each joist.

Position the remaining decking boards with the ends overhanging the end joists. Leave a ⅛" gap between boards to provide for drainage, and attach the boards to each joist with a pair of deck screws.

Every few rows of decking, measure from the edge of the decking to the outside edge of the deck. If the measurement can be divided evenly by 5⅝, the last board will fit flush with the outside edge of the deck as intended. If the measurement shows that the last board will not fit flush, adjust the spacing as you install the remaining rows of boards.

If your decking overhangs the end joists, snap a chalk line to mark the outside edge of the deck and cut flush with a circular saw. If needed, finish the cut with a jigsaw or handsaw where a circular saw can't reach.

BUILD THE STAIRWAY

Refer to the Framing Plan, page 82, for the position of the stairway footings.

Locate the footings by extending a 2 × 4 from the deck, dropping a plumb bob, and marking the centerpoints with stakes.

Dig post holes with a clamshell digger or an auger, and pour the stairway footings using the same method as for the deck footings.

Attach metal post anchors to the footings, and install posts (H), leaving them long for final trimming.

Cut the stair stringers (I) to length and use a framing square to mark the rise and run for each step (see Stairway Detail, page 83). Draw the tread outline on each run. Cut the angles at the end of the stringers with a circular saw. (For more information on building stairways, see pages 50 to 67.)

After attaching the stringers to the deck, fasten them to the posts. Drill and counterbore two pilot holes through the stringers into the posts, and attach with lag screws.

Position a 1½ × 10" angle bracket flush with the bottom of each tread line. Attach the brackets with 1¼" lag screws.

Fasten angle brackets to the upper ends of the stringers, using 1¼" lag screws; keep the brackets flush with cut ends on stringers. Position the top ends of the stringers on the side of the deck, making sure the top point of the stringer and the surface of the deck are flush.

Attach the stringers by driving 10d joist hanger nails through the angle brackets into the end joist, and by drilling ¼" pilot holes from inside the rim joist into the stringers and fastening with ⅜ × 4" lag screws.

To connect the stringers to the stair posts, drill two ¼" pilot holes and counterbore the pilot holes ½" deep with a 1" spade bit. Use a ratchet wrench to fasten the stringers to the posts with 4" lag screws and washers.

Measure the length of the stair treads (J) and cut two 2 × 6 boards for each tread. For each tread, position the front board on the angle bracket so the front edge is flush with the tread outline on the stringers. Attach the tread to the brackets with ¼ × 1¼" lag screws.

Place the rear 2 × 6 on each tread bracket, keeping a ⅛" space between the boards. Attach with 1¼" lag screws.

Attach the treads for the lowest step by driving deck screws through the stringers.

INSTALL THE RAILING

Cut posts (K) and balusters (L) to length (see Railing Detail, page 83) with a power miter saw or circular saw. Cut the top ends square, and the bottom ends at a 45° angle.

Mark and drill two ¼" pilot holes at the bottom end of each post. Holes should be spaced 4" apart and counterbored ½", with a 1" spade bit.

Drill two ⅛" pilot holes, 4" apart, near the bottom of each baluster. At the top of each baluster, drill a pair of ⅛" pilot holes spaced 1½" apart.

Using a combination square, mark the locations of the posts on the outside of the deck. *Note: Position corner posts so there is no more than 4" clearance between them.*

Clamp each post in place. Keep the beveled end flush with the bottom of the deck, and make sure the post is plumb. Use an awl to mark pilot hole locations on the side of the deck. Remove posts and drill ¼" pilot holes at marks. Attach the railing posts to the side of the deck with ⅜ × 5" lag screws and washers.

Position the rail cap over the posts and balusters. Make sure mitered corners are tight, and attach with deck screws.

Cut top rails (M) to length, with 45° miters on the ends that meet at the corners. Attach to posts with 2½" deck screws, keeping the top edge of the rail flush with the top of the posts. Join rails by cutting 45° bevels at ends.

Temporarily attach stairway top rails with 3" galvanized screws. Mark the outline of the deck railing post and top rail on the back side of the stairway top rail. Mark the position of the top rail on the stairway post. Use a level to mark a plumb cutoff line at the lower end of the rail. Remove the rail.

Cut the stairway post to finished height along the diagonal mark, and cut the stairway rail along outlines. Reposition the stairway rail and attach with deck screws.

Attach the balusters between the railing posts at equal intervals of 4" or less. Use deck screws, and keep the top ends of balusters flush with the top rail. On the stairway, position the balusters against the stringer and top rail, and check for plumb. Draw a diagonal cut line at top of baluster and trim to final height with a power miter saw.

Confirm measurements, and cut rail cap sections (N) to length. Position sections so that the inside edge overhangs the inside edge of the rail by ¼". Attach cap to rail with deck screws. At corners, miter the ends 45° and attach caps to posts.

Cut the cap for stairway rail to length. Mark angle of deck railing post on side of cap and bevel-cut the ends of the cap. Attach cap to top rail and post with deck screws. *Note: Local building codes may require a grippable handrail. Check with your building inspector.*

13. Second-story Walkout Deck

This simple rectangular deck provides a secure, convenient outdoor living space. The absence of a stairway prevents children from wandering away or unexpected visitors from wandering in. It also makes the deck easier to build.

Imagine how handy it will be to have this additional living area only a step away from your dining room or living room, with no more need to walk downstairs for outdoor entertaining, dining or relaxing.

And if you'd like to add a stairway, just refer to the chapter on stair-building (see page 50).

Simplicity, security, and convenience are the hallmarks of this elevated deck.

Cutaway View

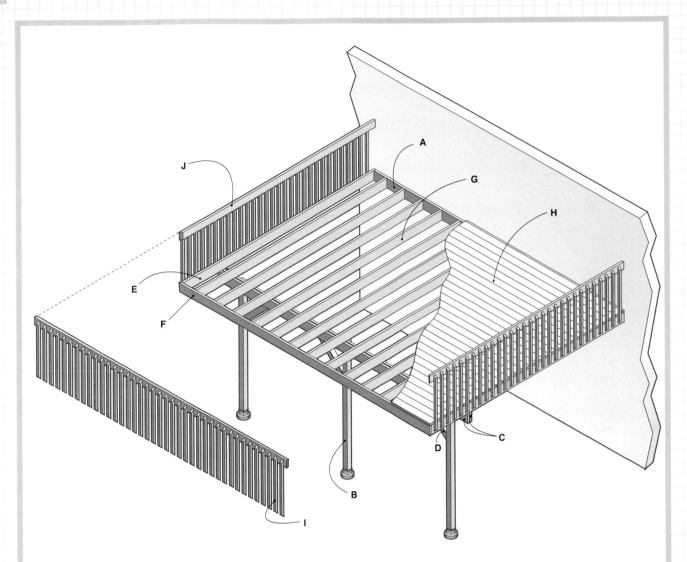

Supplies

12"-diameter footing forms (3)
J-bolts (3)
6 × 6" metal post anchors (3)
2 × 10" joist hangers (26)
Galvanized deck screws (3", 2½" and 1¼")
Joist hanger nails
⅜ × 4" lag screws and washers (28)
¼ × 5" lag screws and washers (16)
⁵⁄₁₆ × 7" carriage bolts, washers, and nuts (6)
16d galvanized nails
Metal flashing (18 ft.)
Silicone caulk (3 tubes)
Concrete as required

Lumber List

Qty.	Size	Material	Part
2	2 × 12" × 20'	Trtd. lumber	Beam boards (C)
2	2 × 10" × 18'	Trtd. lumber	Ledger (A), Rim joist (F)
15	2 × 10" × 14'	Trtd. lumber	Joists (G), End joists (E)
3	6 × 6" × 10'	Trtd. lumber	Deck posts (B)
2	4 × 4" × 8'	Trtd. lumber	Braces (D)
32	2 × 6" × 18'	Cedar	Decking (H), Top rail (J)
2	2 × 6" × 16'	Cedar	Top rail (J)
50	2 × 2" × 8'	Cedar	Balusters (I)

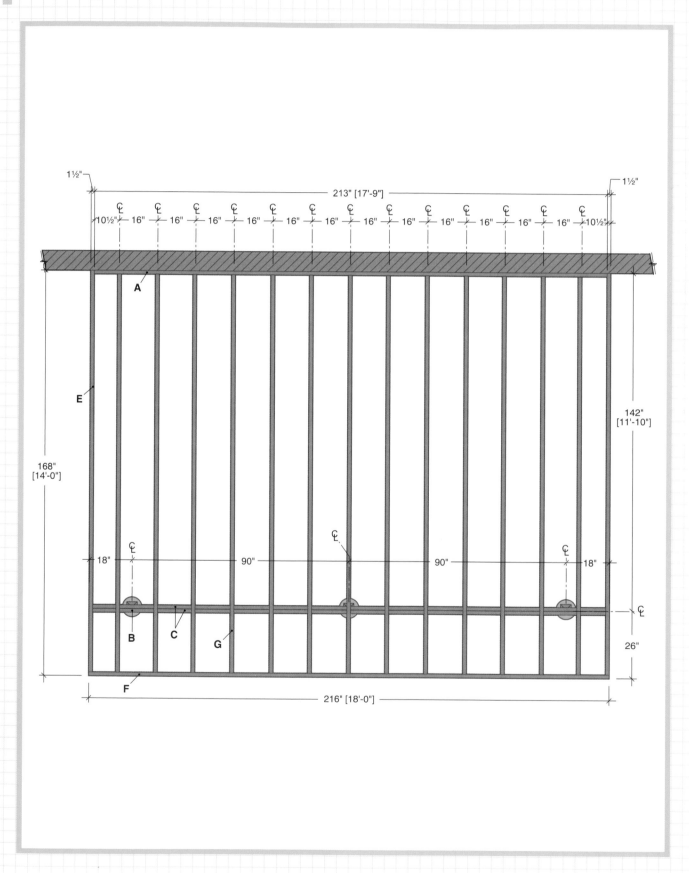

Elevation

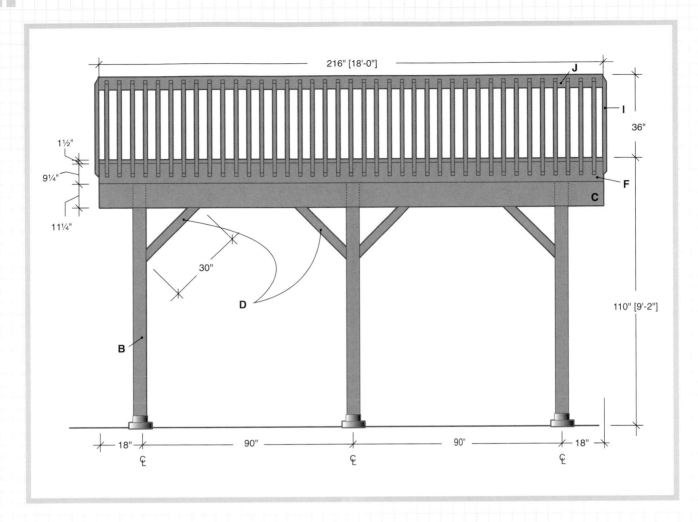

216" [18'-0"]

J

I

36"

F

C

1½"

9¼"

11¼"

30"

D

B

110" [9'-2"]

18"   90"   90"   18"

Railing Detail

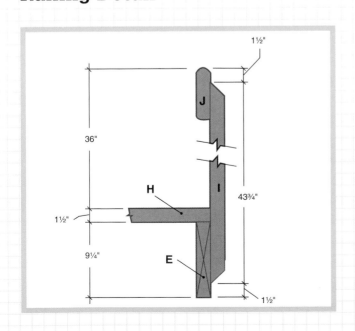

1½"

J

36"

H

I

43¾"

1½"

9¼"

E

1½"

Face Board Detail

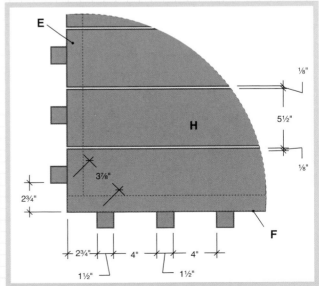

E

⅛"

H

5½"

⅛"

3⅞"

2¾"

F

2¾"   4"   4"

1½"   1½"

How to Build a Second-story Walkout Deck

ATTACH THE LEDGER

Draw a level outline on the siding to show where the ledger and the end joists will fit against the house. Install the ledger so that the surface of the decking boards will be 1" below the indoor floor level. This height difference prevents rainwater or melted snow from seeping into the house.

Cut out the siding along the outline with a circular saw. To avoid cutting the sheathing that lies underneath the siding, set the blade depth to the same thickness as the siding. Finish the cutout with a chisel, holding the beveled side in to ensure a straight cut.

Cut galvanized flashing to the length of the cutout, using metal snips. Slide the flashing up under the siding at the top of the cutout.

Measure and cut the ledger (A) from pressure-treated lumber. Center the ledger end to end in the cutout, with space at each end for the end joist.

Brace the ledger into position under the flashing. Tack the ledger into place with galvanized nails.

Drill pairs of ¼" pilot holes at 16" intervals through the ledger and into the house header joist. Counterbore each pilot hole ½", using a 1" spade bit. Attach the ledger with 4" lag screws and washers, using a ratchet wrench.

Apply silicone caulk between the siding and flashing. Also seal the lag screw heads and the cracks at the ends of the ledger.

POUR THE FOOTINGS

To establish a reference point for locating the footings, drop a plumb bob from the ends of the ledger down to the ground.

Position a straight 14 ft.-long 2 × 4 perpendicular to the house at the point where the plumb bob meets the ground. *Note: If you are building on a steep slope or uneven ground, the mason's string method of locating footing positions will work better (see pages 14 to 19).*

Check for square, using the 3-4-5 triangle method. From the 2 × 4, measure 3 ft. along the wall and make a mark. Next, measure 4 ft. out from the house and make a mark on the 2 × 4. The diagonal line between the marks will measure 5 ft. when the board is accurately square to the house. Adjust the board as needed, using stakes to hold it in place.

Extend another reference board from the house at the other end of the ledger, following the same procedure.

Measure out along both boards, and mark the centerline of the footings (see Framing Plan, page 90).

Lay a straight 2 × 4 between the centerline marks, and drive stakes to mark the footing locations.

Remove the boards and dig the post footings, using a clamshell digger or power auger. Pour 2" to 3" of loose gravel into each hole for drainage. *Note: When measuring the footing size and depth, make sure you comply with local building codes, which may require flaring the base to 18".*

Use a template made from 2 × 4s to locate the post footings on the ground, then mark the footings with stakes.

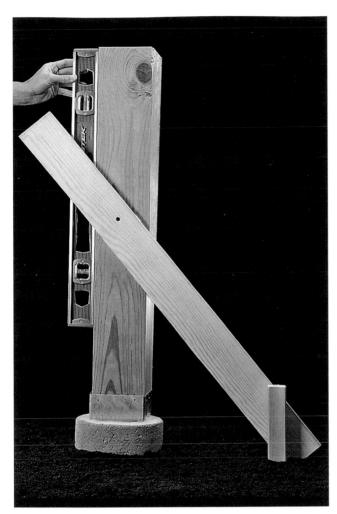

Plumb each post with a level, then use braces and stakes to hold in place until the beam and joists are installed.

Cut the footing forms to length, using a reciprocating saw or handsaw, and insert them into the footing holes, leaving 2" above ground level. Pack soil around the forms for support, and fill the forms with concrete, tamping with a long stick or rod to eliminate any air gaps.

Screed the tops flush with a straight 2 × 4. Insert a J-bolt into the center of each footing and set with ¼" to 1" of thread exposed. Clean the bolt threads before the concrete sets.

SET THE POSTS

Lay a long, straight 2 × 4 flat across the footings, parallel to the house. With one edge tight against the J-bolts, draw a reference line across the top of each footing to help orient the post anchors.

Place a metal post anchor on each footing, centering it over the J-bolt and squaring it with

the reference line. Attach the post anchors by threading a nut over each bolt and tightening with a ratchet wrench.

The tops of the posts (B) will eventually be level with the bottom edge of the ledger, but initially cut the posts several inches longer to allow for final trimming. Position the posts in the anchors and tack into place with one nail each.

With a level as a guide, use braces and stakes to ensure that the posts are plumb.

Determine the height of the beam by using a chalk line and a line level. Extend the chalk line out from the bottom edge of the ledger, make sure that the line is level, and snap a mark across the face of a post. Use the line and level to transfer the mark to the remaining posts.

NOTCH THE POSTS

Remove the posts from the post anchors and cut to the finished height.

Measure and mark a 3" × 11¼" notch at the top of each post, on the outside face. Use a framing square to trace lines on all sides. Rough-cut the notches with a circular saw, then finish with a reciprocating saw or handsaw.

Reattach the posts to the post anchors, with the notch-side facing away from the deck.

INSTALL THE BEAM

Cut the beam boards (C) to length, adding several inches to each end for final trimming after the deck frame is squared up.

Join the beam boards together with 2½" galvanized deck screws. Mark the post locations on the top edges and sides, using a combination square as a guide.

Lift the beam, one end at a time, into the notches with the crown up. Align and clamp the beam to the posts. *Note: Installing boards of this size and length, at this height, requires caution. You should have at least two helpers.*

Counterbore two ½"-deep holes using a 1" spade bit, then drill ⁵⁄₁₆" pilot holes through the beam and post.

Thread a carriage bolt into each pilot hole. Add a washer and nut to the counterbore-side of each bolt and tighten with a ratchet wrench. Seal both ends of the bolts with silicone caulk.

Cut the tops of the posts flush with the top edge of the beam, using a reciprocating saw or handsaw.

(continued)

INSTALL THE FRAME

Measure and cut the end joists (E) to length, using a circular saw.

Attach the end joists to the ends of the ledger with 16d galvanized nails.

Measure and cut the rim joist (F) to length with a circular saw. Fasten to the ends of end joists with 16d nails.

Square up the frame by measuring corner to corner and adjusting until the measurements are equal. When the frame is square, toenail the end joists in place on top of the beam.

Trim the ends of the beam flush with the faces of the end joists, using a reciprocating saw or a handsaw.

INSTALL THE BRACES

Cut the braces (D) to length (see Elevation, page 91) with a circular saw or power miter saw. Miter both ends at 45°.

Install the braces by positioning them against the beam boards and against the posts. Make sure the outside faces of the braces are flush with the outside faces of the beam and the posts. Temporarily fasten with deck screws.

Secure the braces to the posts with 5" lag screws. Drill two ¼" pilot holes through the upper end of each brace into the beam. Counterbore to a ½"-depth using a 1" spade bit, and drive lag screws with a ratchet wrench. Repeat for the lower end of the braces into the posts.

Snap a chalk line flush with the outside edge of the deck, and cut off overhanging deck boards with a circular saw.

After cutting balusters to length, gang them up and drill ⅛" pilot holes through the top and bottom.

INSTALL THE JOISTS

Measure and mark the joist locations (see Framing Plan, page 90) on the ledger, rim joist, and beam. Draw the outline of each joist on the ledger and rim joist, using a combination square.

Install a joist hanger at each joist location. Attach one flange of the hanger to one side of the outline, using joist nails. Use a spacer cut from scrap 2 × 8 lumber to achieve the correct spread for each hanger, then fasten the remaining side flange with joist nails. Remove the spacer and repeat the same procedure for the remaining joist hangers.

Measure, mark, and cut lumber for joists (G), using a circular saw. Place joists in hangers with crown side up and attach with joist hanger nails. Align joists with the outlines on the top of the beam, and toenail in place.

LAY THE DECKING

Measure, mark, and cut the decking boards (H) to length as needed.

Position the first row of decking flush against the house, and attach by driving a pair of galvanized deck screws into each joist.

Position the remaining decking boards, leaving a ⅛" gap between boards to provide for drainage, and attach to each joist with deck screws.

Every few rows of decking, measure from the edge of the decking to the outside edge of the deck. If the measurement can be divided evenly by 5⅝", the last board will fit flush with the outside edge of the deck as intended. If the measurement shows that the last board will not fit flush, adjust the spacing as you install the remaining rows of boards.

If your decking overhangs the end joists, snap a chalk line to mark the outside edge of the deck and cut flush with a circular saw set to a 1½" depth. If needed, finish the cut with a jigsaw or handsaw where a circular saw can't reach.

BUILD THE RAILING

Measure, mark, and cut the balusters (I) to length, with 45° miters at both ends.

Gang the balusters together and drill two ⅛" pilot holes at both ends.

Clamp a 1½" guide strip flush with the bottom edge of the deck platform to establish the baluster height (see Railing Detail, page 91).

To ensure that the balusters are installed at equal intervals, create a spacing jig, less than 4" wide, from two pieces of scrap material.

To make a joint in the top rail, cut the ends at 45° and drill a pair of pilot holes. Then fasten the ends together with deck screws.

Attach the corner balusters first (see Face Board Detail, page 91), using a level to ensure that they are plumb. Then use the spacing jig for positioning, and attach the remaining balusters to the deck platform with 3" deck screws.

Measure, mark, and cut the top rail sections (J) to length. Round over three edges (see Railing Detail, page 91) using a router with a ½" round-over bit. Cut 45° miters on the ends that meet at the corners.

Hold or clamp the top rail in position, and attach with 2½" deck screws driven through the balusters.

If you need to make straight joints in the top rail, cut the ends of the adjoining boards at 45°. Drill angled ⅛" pilot holes and join with deck screws.

Creative Publishing
international

Copyright © 2010
Creative Publishing international, Inc.
400 First Avenue North, Suite 300
Minneapolis, Minnesota 55401
1-800-328-0590
www.creativepub.com

Printed at R.R. Donnelley

10 9 8 7 6 5 4 3 2 1

Here's How Decks
Created by: The Editors of Creative Publishing international, Inc., in cooperation with Black & Decker. Black & Decker® is a trademark of The Black & Decker Corporation and is used under license.

President/CEO: Ken Fund
VP for Sales & Marketing: Kevin Hamric

Home Improvement Group

Publisher: Bryan Trandem
Managing Editor: Tracy Stanley
Senior Editor: Mark Johanson
Editor: Jennifer Gehlhar

Creative Director: Michele Lanci-Altomare
Senior Design Managers: Jon Simpson, Brad Springer
Design Manager: James Kegley

Lead Photographer: Joel Schnell

Production Managers: Linda Halls, Laura Hokkanen

Page Layout Artist: Katie Yokiel